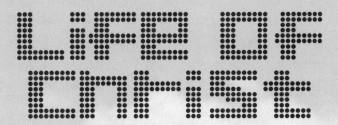

GROUP directory

Pass this Directory around and have your Group Members
fill in their names and phone numbers

Name   Phone

_____   _____

_____   _____

_____   _____

_____   _____

_____   _____

_____   _____

_____   _____

_____   _____

_____   _____

_____   _____

_____   _____

_____   _____

_____   _____

_____   _____

_____   _____

_____   _____

_____   _____

_____   _____

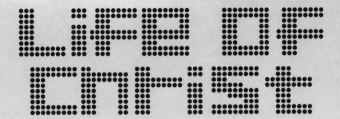

LIFE OF CHRIST

EDITING AND PRODUCTION TEAM:

James F. Couch, Jr., Lyman Coleman, Sharon Penington, Cathy Tardif,
Christopher Werner, Matthew Lockhart, Erika Tiepel, Richard Peace,
Andrew Sloan, Mike Shepherd, Margaret Harris, Scott Lee, Gregory C. Benoit

SERENDIPITY
HOUSE

NASHVILLE, TENNESSEE

Life of Christ
© 1988, 1998, 2003 Serendipity House
Reprinted March 2007

Published by Serendipity House Publishers
Nashville, Tennessee

ISBN: 978-1-5749-4316-0

To purchase additional copies of this resource or other studies:
ORDER ONLINE at www.SerendipityHouse.com
WRITE Serendipity House, 117 10th Avenue North, Nashville, TN 37234
FAX (615) 277-8181
PHONE (800) 525-9563

1-800-525-9563
www.SerendipityHouse.com

Printed in the United States of America
12 11 10 09 08 07   2 3 4 5 6 7 8 9 10

table of contents

SESSION	REFERENCE	SUBJECT	PAGE
1	Luke 2:1–20	The Birth of Jesus	11
2	Matthew 3:13–4:11	The Baptist and Temptation	19
3	Luke 4:14–30	Jesus' Early Ministry	25
4	John 1:35–51	Jesus Calls His Disciples	31
5	Mark 2:13–22; 3:1–6	Jesus and the Religious Leaders	37
6	Matthew 9:18–34	Jesus Heals	43
7	Mark 8:27–38	Jesus the Messiah	49
8	Mark 9:2–13	Jesus and the Transfiguration	55
9	Mark 14:12–26	Jesus and the Last Supper	61
10	Mark 14:32–42	Jesus in Gethsemane	67
11	Mark 15:1–20	Jesus Before Pilate	73
12	Mark 15:22–41	Jesus' Crucifixion	79
13	Matthew 28:1–20	The Resurrection of Jesus	85

CORE VALUES

Community: The purpose of this curriculum is to build community within the body of believers around Jesus Christ.

Group Process: To build community, the curriculum must be designed to take a group through a step-by-step process of sharing your story with one another.

Interactive Bible Study: To share your "story," the approach to Scripture in the curriculum needs to be open-ended and right brain—to "level the playing field" and encourage everyone to share.

Developmental Stages: To provide a healthy program throughout the four stages of the life cycle of a group, the curriculum needs to offer courses on three levels of commitment: (1) Beginner Level—low-level entry, high structure, to level the playing field; (2) Growth Level—deeper Bible study, flexible structure, to encourage group accountability; (3) Discipleship Level—in-depth Bible study, open structure, to move the group into high gear.

Target Audiences: To build community throughout the culture of the church, the curriculum needs to be flexible, adaptable and transferable into the structure of the average church.

Mission: To expand the kingdom of God one person at a time by filling the "empty chair." (We add an extra chair to each group session to remind us of our mission.)

introduction

Each healthy small group will move through various stages as it matures.

Multiply Stage: The group begins the multiplication process. Members pray about their involvement in new groups. The "new" groups begin the life cycle again with the Birth Stage.

Birth Stage: This is the time in which group members form relationships and begin to develop community. The group will spend more time in ice-breaker exercises, relational Bible study and covenant building.

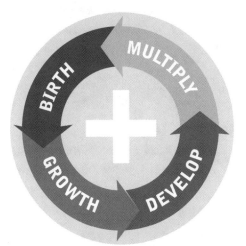

Develop Stage: The inductive Bible study deepens while the group members discover and develop gifts and skills. The group explores ways to invite their neighbors and coworkers to group meetings.

Growth Stage: Here the group begins to care for one another as it learns to apply what they learn through Bible study, worship and prayer.

Subgrouping: If you have nine or more people at a meeting, Serendipity recommends you divide into subgroups of 3–6 for the Bible study. Ask one person to be the leader of each subgroup and to follow the directions for the Bible study. After 30 minutes, the Group Leader will call "time" and ask all subgroups to come together for the Caring Time.

Each group meeting should include all parts of the "three-part agenda."

 Ice-Breaker: Fun, history-giving questions are designed to warm the group and to build understanding about the other group members. You can choose to use all of the Ice-Breaker questions, especially if there is a new group member that will need help in feeling comfortable with the group.

 Bible Study: The heart of each meeting is the reading and examination of the Bible. The questions are open, discover questions that lead to further inquiry. Reference notes are provided to give everyone a "level playing field." The emphasis is on understanding what the Bible says and applying the truth to real life. The questions for each session build. There is always at least one "going deeper" question provided. You should always leave time for the last of the "questions for interaction." Should you choose, you can use the optional "going deeper" question to satisfy the desire for the challenging questions in groups that have been together for a while.

 **Caring Time:** All study should point us to actions. Each session ends with prayer and direction in caring for the needs of the group members. You can choose between several questions. You should always pray for the "empty chair." Who do you know that could fill that void in your group?

Sharing Your Story: These sessions are designed for members to share a little of their personal lives each time. Through a number of special techniques, each member is encouraged to move from low risk, less personal sharing to higher risk responses. This helps develop the sense of community and facilitates caregiving.

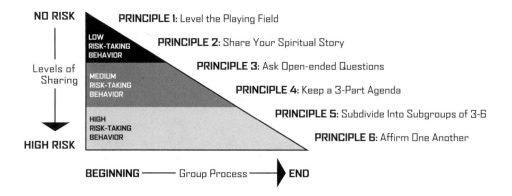

NO RISK

PRINCIPLE 1: Level the Playing Field

LOW RISK-TAKING BEHAVIOR

PRINCIPLE 2: Share Your Spiritual Story

PRINCIPLE 3: Ask Open-ended Questions

Levels of Sharing

MEDIUM RISK-TAKING BEHAVIOR

PRINCIPLE 4: Keep a 3-Part Agenda

PRINCIPLE 5: Subdivide Into Subgroups of 3-6

HIGH RISK-TAKING BEHAVIOR

PRINCIPLE 6: Affirm One Another

HIGH RISK

BEGINNING ——— Group Process ——▶ END

Group Covenant: A group covenant is a "contract" that spells out your expectations and the ground rules for your group. It's very important that your group discuss these issues–preferably as part of the first session.

GROUND RULES:

• Priority: While you are in the group, you give the group meeting priority.

• Participation: Everyone participates and no one dominates.

• Respect: Everyone is given the right to their own opinion and all questions are encouraged and respected.

• Confidentiality: Anything that is said in the meeting is never repeated outside the meeting.

• Empty Chair: The group stays open to new people at every meeting.

• Support: Permission is given to call upon each other in time of need–even in the middle of the night.

• Advice Giving: Unsolicited advice is not allowed.

• Mission: We agree to do everything in our power to start a new group as our mission.

GOALS:

• The time and place this group is going to meet is_____.

• Refreshments are _____ responsibility.

• Child care is _____ responsibility.

SESSION 1 : THE BIRTH OF JESUS

SCRIPTURE LUKE 2:1–20

In spite of Jesus' great influence, however, there is still a sense of mystery surrounding him. Who was Jesus? What was he like? We will turn to the Gospels to help us answer these questions. The Gospels were not written merely as histories of Jesus. We simply do not have an untouched history of the life of Jesus. But what we do have are four Spirit-inspired character sketches of his life, teachings and significance.

Studies in this book should not be approached as a "harmony" of the Gospels. While the material has been arranged in a logical order (beginning with Luke's birth story and ending with Matthew's account of the Resurrection), the point is not to try to present a history of Jesus. Instead, these studies are more like snapshots in a photograph album. Each snapshot tells an important story about Jesus. The main purpose of these passages is to lead readers into a greater understanding of the meaning of Jesus' life and its implications for their own. What may start as an interest in a famous person of history it becomes an exercise in self-evaluation and decision making.

We will each personally have to wrestle with the question, "Who is Jesus?" We will especially have to confront the ways in which our views of Jesus are more colored by our particular culture than by the meaning of the stories we have about him. We will also have to wrestle with our response to Jesus. Too often people look to the Gospels (and the Bible as a whole) only as a source of comfort and assurance. In reality, a great deal of the Bible is meant to provoke precisely the opposite reactions.

The Gospels do not give us the option of holding a polite, distant admiration of Jesus as a wonderful religious teacher. Instead, they call for us to think and live differently. We have to change, and be ready to keep on changing as the implications of discipleship unfold before us and become clear. A continual, thoughtful reading of the Gospels will not reinforce any long-held image of Jesus. The picture is more like looking at an object through a kaleidoscope. We will find a dynamic, multi-faceted character whose identity and teaching cannot be captured by any one description. Reading and reflecting upon the life of Jesus is a dangerous habit. It will continually force us to deal with the basic challenge of the Christian faith: In light of what you understand about Jesus, how will you follow him now?

ICE-BREAKER : CONNECT WITH YOUR GROUP | 15 MINUTES

LEADER: Be sure to read the introductory material in the front of this book prior to this first session. To help your group members get acquainted, have each person introduce him or herself and then take turns answering one or two of the Ice-Breaker questions. If time allows, you may want to discuss all three questions.

Today we are beginning our journey through the life of Christ with a look at his birth and his name. Names held great meaning in those days, but today we often forget that names have meanings. Take some time to get to know one another better by sharing your responses to the following questions.

1. Tell us about yourself: When and where were you born? Do you have any siblings? What are their names and gender?

2. What does your name mean? If you have children, why did you give them the names you gave them?

3. If you were out camping and some angels appeared in the sky above you, what would you think?
   ❑ "What was in that stew?"
   ❑ "I am now going to die."
   ❑ "I must be in heaven."
   ❑ "Get a camera."
   ❑ "Come on down, I have lots of questions."
   ❑ I would be speechless.
   ❑ Other _____.

BIBLE STUDY : READ SCRIPTURE AND DISCUSS | 30 MINUTES

LEADER: Select two members of the group ahead of time to read aloud the Scripture passage. Then discuss the Questions for Interaction, dividing into subgroups of three to six. Be sure to save time at the end for the Caring Time.

Regardless of what you believe about him, there is one event on this earth that has changed history forever: the birth of Jesus Christ. He was born into poverty to a virgin girl. Shepherds were some of the first to seek him out, and people have been seeking him ever since. Let's read Luke 2:1–20 to gain an understanding of the importance of this event for us and for our world.

The Birth of Jesus

Reader One:

2 In those days a decree went out from Caesar Augustus that the whole empire should be registered. ²This first registration took place while Quirinius was governing Syria. ³So everyone went to be registered, each to his own town.

⁴And Joseph also went up from the town of Nazareth in Galilee, to Judea, to the city of David, which is called Bethlehem, because he was of the house and family line of David, ⁵to be registered along with Mary, who was engaged to him and was preg-

nant. ⁶While they were there, it happened that the days were completed for her to give birth. ⁷Then she gave birth to her first-born Son, and she wrapped Him snugly in cloth and laid Him in a manger—because there was no room for them at the inn.

⁸In the same region, shepherds were living out in the fields and keeping watch at night over their flock. ⁹Then an angel of the Lord stood before them, and the glory of the Lord shone around them, and they were terrified. ¹⁰But the angel said to them,

Reader Two: "Do not be afraid, for you see, I announce to you good news of great joy that will be for all the people: ¹¹because today in the city of David was born for you a Savior, who is Christ the Lord. ¹²This will be the sign for you: you will find a baby wrapped snugly in cloth and lying in a manger."

Reader One: ¹³Suddenly there was a multitude of the heavenly host with the angel, praising God and saying:

Reader Two: ¹⁴Glory to God in the highest heaven, and peace on earth to people He favors

Reader One: ¹⁵When the angels had left them and returned to heaven, the shepherds said to one another,

Reader Two: "Let's go straight to Bethlehem and see this thing that has taken place, which the Lord has made known to us."

Reader One: ¹⁶And they hurried off and found both Mary and Joseph, and the baby who was lying in the manger. ¹⁷After seeing them, they reported the message they were told about this child, ¹⁸and all who heard it were amazed at what the shepherds said to them. ¹⁹But Mary was treasuring up all these things in her heart and meditating on them. ²⁰The shepherds returned, glorifying and praising God for all they had seen and heard, just as they had been told.

                                                              Luke 2:1–20

LEADER: Refer to the Summary and Study Notes at the end of this session as needed. If 30 minutes is not enough time to answer all of the questions in this section, conclude the Bible Study by answering questions 6 and 7.

1. What are some common negative comments today of young girls who get pregnant out of wedlock?
   - ❏ That poor girl.
   - ❏ Who is the father?
   - ❏ She will never make it.
   - ❏ You reap what you sow.
   - ❏ Other _____.

   What do you think the religious people thought about Mary and her situation?

2. How did Mary and Joseph travel from Nazareth to Bethlehem? How do you think Mary felt about that trip?

3. Why was it important for Jesus to be born in Bethlehem, in a cave and in a manger? What was the significance of this (Mic. 5:2)?

4. Why do you suppose the shepherds were some of the first to hear about Jesus' birth? Why did they glorify God when they went back to their fields? What had they seen that affected them this way?

5. What was the significance of the three titles the angels attributed to Jesus in verse 11?

6. On what do you think Mary was meditating, as mentioned in verse 19? What do you treasure most about Jesus?

7. What is your response to Jesus' birth?
   - ❏ I want to tell others about it, as the shepherds did.
   - ❏ I need to take time to meditate on it, as Mary did.
   - ❏ I love to praise God for it, as the angels did.
   - ❏ Other _____.

GOING DEEPER:

If your group has time and/or wants a challenge, go on to this question.

8. What is meant by the phrase, "peace on earth to people He favors" (v. 14)?

CARING TIME : APPLY THE LESSON AND PRAY FOR ONE ANOTHER | 15 MIN.

LEADER: Take some extra time in this first session to go over the introductory material at the beginning of this book. At the close, pass around your books and have everyone sign the Group Directory in the front of this book.

This is an important time for expressing your concern for each other through prayer.

1. Agree on the group covenant and ground rules that are described in the introduction to this book.

2. Why did you decide to join this study on the life of Christ? What do you hope to gain?

3. Share any other prayer requests and praises, and then close in prayer. Pray specifically for God to bring someone into your life next week to fill the empty chair.

NEXT WEEK

Today we explored the meaning of the birth of Jesus. He entered this world as the Savior, the Christ and the Lord for all who will believe. In the coming week, take some extra time to thank God for sending his Son into the world for your salvation. Next week we will continue to follow the journey of Jesus' life as we look at his baptism and temptation.

Summary: Luke roots Jesus' birth firmly in history. Augustus ruled the Roman Empire from 30 B.C. to A.D. 14. Originally known as Gaius Octavius (or Octavian), he was awarded the title Augustus (which means "majestic" or "highly revered") by the Roman senate and became known thereafter as Caesar Augustus. Augustus was a wise ruler who encouraged the arts and built many fine projects. He also brought an unprecedented period of peace to the world. From about 30 B.C. onward, the Caesars ordered people in the various Roman provinces to report every 14 years for a census for purposes of taxation. Resistance from the population and from local rulers sometimes meant census-taking required several years to complete. A census was connected with Quirinius for both of his terms of office, 6–4 B.C. and 6–9 A.D. The first census was the one connected with Jesus birth; Acts 5:37 refers to the second census.

2:3 each to his own town. Since Joseph and Mary lived in Galilee, they must have owned some property in Bethlehem. Roman custom required people who owned property in another location than where they lived to register there as well. Bethlehem, a three to four-day journey from Galilee, was the village where King David, through whose line the Messiah was to come, had lived.

2:4 Bethlehem. Bethlehem was some 90 miles from Nazareth, a three or four-day journey. Joseph was from the line of David and Bethlehem was the city of David, so this is where Joseph's family and clan would have lived (which is why he would have had property there).

2:5 to be registered along with Mary. Normally only the head of the household needed to register. However, in some Roman provinces all women over 12 were required to pay a poll tax, and this may have been the reason Mary accompanied Joseph on this trip. **engaged to him and was pregnant.** Their betrothal had not yet been consummated by intercourse (Matt. 1:24–25). Luke records the announcement by the angel to Mary that she would conceive a child through the agency of the Holy Spirit (1:26–38).

2:7 firstborn. The firstborn of every Jewish family was dedicated to God in a special way (Ex. 13:12). This firstborn son would be dedicated in a way unlike any other child. **she wrapped Him snugly in cloth.** The tradition of the time was to wrap a baby in strips of cloth. Such cloths would give the child the feeling of being securely held. **manger.** A feeding trough for animals. **the inn.** This can mean either a building used for the accommodation of travelers or a spare room in a private home. Whichever the case, there was no space for the couple, who stayed instead with the animals. A tradition dating back to the second century maintains this was in a cave over which today is the Church of the Nativity

2:8 shepherds. Shepherds were economically and religiously "low-class" people. Since temple authorities kept flocks of sheep for sacrificial purposes pastured near Bethlehem, it might be that the shepherds of these particular flocks were the ones visited by the angels. So it was to shepherds that the great announcement was made—not to kings nor to priests nor to the wealthy nor even to the religious—but it was to lower-class working men that the angel of the Lord appeared to announce the birth of the Savior. This happened at a time of year when sheep could still be kept in the field, which was sometime between April and

November. The date of December 25 as the birth of Christ was selected in the fourth century. It was the occasion of a pagan festival associated with the rebirth of various solar deities, and was the date of the winter solstice according to the Julian calendar.

2:9 an angel of the Lord. In some Old Testament passages, the angel of the Lord is virtually identified as God himself (Gen. 16:7ff; Ex. 3:2; Judg. 6:11ff), indicating his divine authority and splendor. Popular thought often pictures angels as chubby, cute, naked children, but the Bible consistently represents them as supernatural creatures of enormous power and majesty. Throughout the Bible, angels serve as God's agents of instruction, judgment and deliverance. **the glory of the Lord.** The overwhelmingly powerful light that accompanies the presence of God (Ps. 104:1–2; Ezek. 1). **they were terrified.** Whenever in the Bible an angel appears to a person, the response is one of terror. It is the fear of being in the presence of something supernatural, powerful and totally foreign to one's experience (1:29–30; Dan. 10:7).

2:10 Do not be afraid. The angel has not come to frighten them, but to announce God's good news to them. **I announce to you good news of great joy.** The form of the angel's message is similar to that used to announce the birth of Roman kings. **all the people.** The Savior has come not just for Jews but for all people. This is an important theme in Luke's gospel. God's mercy includes the Gentiles, the Gospel is universal, not particular.

2:11 a Savior ... Christ the Lord. A "Savior," a term in the Old Testament which only applies to God, is one who delivers his people from evil and harm. "Christ" means one anointed by God to rule. "Lord" implies both his authority and deity. **Savior.** In the Old Testament, this term only applied to God (Isa. 43:3,11). God's deliverance of Israel (first from Egypt and then, centuries later, from Babylon) illustrates that the title is meant to honor God as the one who rescues his people from an otherwise unbeatable foe. This title was ascribed to Jesus as the one who saves his people from sin and death. **Christ.** This is the Greek word for the Hebrew title, Messiah. Both terms mean "the Anointed One." In Jewish thought, this meant the prophesied king of Israel who would deliver Israel from bondage into an era of freedom, power, influence and prosperity. **Lord.** This is a very common title used for God in the Old Testament. It implies both his absolute authority and his deity. In the New Testament, this is the most often used title for Jesus as well, emphasizing his deity and authority.

2:12 the sign. In the Old Testament, God sometimes granted signs that pointed out to people the reliability of his message. The "sign" of the Lord is, strangely enough, that of a baby wrapped in cloths and lying in an animal's feeding trough.

2:13 At a birth, neighbors and friends would gather to celebrate. At this birth, while Mary and Joseph are away from family, and possibly shamed by friends, the angels fulfill this function. **multitude of the heavenly host.** The angels, who were close to God, were intensely interested in the advent of Christ and the way that God would redeem human beings. The angels longed to "look into these things," (1 Peter 1:12), speaking of salvation, grace, and the suffering of the anointed one who was foretold by the prophets.

2:14 Glory to God in the highest heaven. The angelic voices proclaim Jesus' birth that will bring honor to God and personal and relational harmony to people whom he has called. **peace on earth to people He favors.** While older versions divide this phrase into two clauses (peace on earth/good will toward men), the single clause accenting God's promise of peace to his people, is to be preferred. There are not two statements of God's wishes for humanity, but a clear promise of peace to those who receive God's grace.

2:17 they reported the message. Luke is concerned throughout his gospel, as well as in Acts, to show that the message of Christ is to be spread to all people. The shepherds become the first witnesses, announcing the Good News of God that is centered in the story of Jesus.

2:19 Mary was treasuring up all these things in her heart and meditating on them. The words used to describe Mary's response indicate deep thought and reflection in an attempt to understand.

2:20 returned, glorifying and praising God. The shepherds' response is similar to the disciples' after the Resurrection and Ascension (24:52–53).

SESSION 2 : THE BAPTISM AND TEMPTATION

SCRIPTURE MATTHEW 3:13–4:11

LAST WEEK

In last week's session, we considered the significance of Jesus' birth. We were reminded that he came as our Savior, Christ and Lord. We also discussed our personal response to Jesus' birth and what we treasure most about him. Today we will examine his identification with humanity through his baptism and temptation.

ICE-BREAKER : CONNECT WITH YOUR GROUP | 15 MINUTES

LEADER: Begin the session with a word of prayer. Have your group members take turns sharing their responses to one, two or all three of the Ice-Breaker questions. Be sure that everyone gets a chance to participate.

We all have to eat to live, but sometimes we need to remind ourselves that we do not live to eat! However, food is one of the pleasures of God's creation, and variety, after all, is the spice of life. Take turns sharing some thoughts about your favorite foods.

1. What is your favorite kind of food?
   - ❏ Fast food.
   - ❏ Italian.
   - ❏ Mexican.
   - ❏ American.
   - ❏ Greek.
   - ❏ Asian.
   - ❏ Other _____.

2. What was your favorite snack when you arrived home from school?

3. What is the longest you've gone without food? How does hunger affect you?

LEADER: Select four members of the group ahead of time to read aloud the Scripture passage. Assign the following parts: Matthew (the narrator), John, Jesus and Satan. Then discuss the Questions for Interaction, dividing into subgroups of three to six.

It was important for Jesus to identity with humanity. If he had not, there could be no salvation of humanity. Two ways he identified with us were in his baptism and in the ways he was tempted to sin but did not sin. Let's read Matthew 3:13–4:11 to gain an understanding of how he identifies with us.

The Baptism and Temptation

Matthew: ¹³Then Jesus came from Galilee to John at the Jordan, to be baptized by him. ¹⁴But John tried to stop Him, saying,

John: "I need to be baptized by You, and yet You come to me?"

Matthew: ¹⁵Jesus answered him,

Jesus: "Allow it for now, because this is the way for us to fulfill all righteousness."

Matthew: Then he allowed Him to be baptized. ¹⁶After Jesus was baptized, He went up immediately from the water. The heavens suddenly opened for Him, and He saw the Spirit of God descending like a dove and coming down on Him. ¹⁷And there came a voice from heaven: "This is My beloved Son. I take delight in Him!"

4 Then Jesus was led up by the Spirit into the wilderness to be tempted by the Devil. ²And after He had fasted 40 days and 40 nights, He was hungry. ³Then the tempter approached Him and said,

Satan: "If You are the Son of God, tell these stones to become bread."

Matthew: ⁴But He answered,

Jesus: "It is written: 'Man must not live on bread alone, but on every word that comes from the mouth of God.' "

Matthew: ⁵Then the Devil took Him to the holy city, had Him stand on the pinnacle of the temple, ⁶and said to Him,

Satan:	"If You are the Son of God, throw Yourself down. For it is written: 'He will give His angels orders concerning you, and, they will support you with their hands, so that you will not strike your foot against a stone.' "
Matthew:	⁷Jesus told him,
Jesus:	"It is also written: 'You must not tempt the Lord your God.' "
Matthew:	⁸Again, the Devil took Him to a very high mountain and showed Him all the kingdoms of the world and their splendor. ⁹And he said to Him,
Satan:	"I will give You all these things if You will fall down and worship me."
Matthew:	¹⁰Then Jesus told him,
Jesus:	"Go away, Satan! For it is written: 'You must worship the Lord your God, and you must serve Him only.' "
Matthew:	¹¹Then the Devil left Him, and immediately angels came and began to serve Him.

Matthew 3:13–4:11

QUESTIONS FOR INTERACTION

LEADER: Refer to the Summary and Study Notes at the end of this session as needed. If 30 minutes is not enough time to answer all of the questions in this section, conclude the Bible Study by answering questions 6 and 7.

1. By what food are you most tempted?
   - ❏ Peanut butter.
   - ❏ Chocolate.
   - ❏ French fries.
   - ❏ Chips.
   - ❏ Cookies.
   - ❏ Other _____.

2. What did Jesus mean in 3:15 when he said "to fulfill all righteousness"? What was the significance of baptism for Jesus? For followers of Christ?

3. If you have been baptized, why did you do it? What does your baptism mean to you?

21

4. What were the three circumstances in which Jesus was tempted? How did he overcome those temptations?

5. What do you learn from the way Jesus dealt with each temptation?

6. Of the three areas with which Satan tempted Jesus, which area do you struggle with the most?
   ❏ Physical struggles (food, sex, appearance, etc.).
   ❏ Pride (self-centeredness, not needing anyone in my life).
   ❏ Power (wanting to control my life, do things my way).

7. What have you found helpful in overcoming temptation? How can we help each other resist Satan and his lies?

GOING DEEPER: If your group has time and/or wants a challenge, go on to this question.

8. What do you think the affirmation of the Father meant to Jesus? How important is affirmation in the discipleship process? How can we affirm one another?

CARING TIME : APPLY THE LESSON AND PRAY FOR ONE ANOTHER | 15 MIN.

LEADER: Bring the group back together and begin the Caring Time by sharing responses to all three questions. Then take turns sharing prayer requests and having a time of group prayer. Be sure to include prayer for the empty chair.

All people face temptations of various kinds. The difference between Christians and non-Christians is that we have the Holy Spirit living within us to guide us and to strengthen us when we are faced with temptation. Almost as important as this is the strength we can gain by leaning on each other during times of temptation. Spend some time now in sharing and prayer, giving support and encouragement to one another.

1. Where are you in the journey of following Christ?

2. This past week, did you feel more victorious or defeated when it came to temptation, and why?

3. How safe do you feel sharing your struggles with this group? How about with an individual within this group?

P.S. Add new group members to the Group Directory at the front of this book.

Today we considered Jesus' baptism and temptation. We were reminded that Jesus knows what it is like to be tempted, so he understands and can help us in our life struggles. We also saw the importance of making this group safe enough for people to share their struggles and still live in community. In the coming week, pray for all of the group members, that each person would be able to overcome temptation with the help of the Holy Spirit. Next week we will continue to follow the journey of Christ's life as we study the beginning of his earthly ministry.

NOTES ON MATTHEW 3:13–4:11

Summary: At that time, only Gentiles who were converting to Judaism had to be baptized (in order to wash away the "Gentile filth" with which they were associated). John's call pointed out that Jews needed cleansing and repentance every bit as much as any Gentile. In 3:11–12, John announces that his ministry is simply the prelude of the One to come, who will baptize people with the Holy Spirit and the fire of God's judgment. He is the one to whom John has been pointing. When Israel was freed from Egypt, the people gave in to sin in the desert. They failed to trust that God would provide food (Ex. 16:1–3). They tested God because they did not believe in his care for them (Ex. 17:1–7). They worshiped other gods in hopes of finding an easier way (Ex. 32). In Jesus' wilderness experience he overcame all these temptations.

3:13 from Galilee to John at the Jordan. This was a journey of a few days. Galilee was a province to the north of where John was baptizing in the Jordan River, in the province of Judea. **baptized.** By allowing himself to be baptized, Jesus both identifies with the sin of his people (prefiguring his death for sin a few years hence) and proclaims his radical allegiance to God (an allegiance that will be tested through his temptations).

3:14 I need to be baptized by You. How John recognized Jesus as the One to come is not mentioned.

3:16 like a dove. Matthew uses the symbol of a dove to communicate the coming of the Holy Spirit. Its meaning is clear: this is the promised anointing of the Messiah with the Holy Spirit (Isa. 11:2; 42:1; 61:1).

3:17 a voice. The words of the voice combined Psalm 2:7 and Isaiah 42:1. **This is My beloved Son.** This phrase is associated with the Suffering Servant of Isaiah (Isa. 42:1) who suffers while carrying out God's will in the service of Israel. In Jesus, the two Old Testament figures of God's Servant and God's royal Son are combined. **I take delight in Him.** This

23

phrase is borrowed from Isaiah 42:1, which speaks of God's delight in his servant. In Isaiah, the servant of the Lord is the one who suffers for the sake of the people. Popular thought of the time did not associate the role of the Messiah with that of the Suffering Servant.

4:1 led by the Spirit. The same Spirit who had come to Jesus in such affirming power, now sends him forth to this time of testing. **tempted.** He endured temptation and did not sin, so that we could have an intercessor who understands everything that we as humans go through. (Heb. 2:18).

4:2 forty days. Moses fasted 40 days on Mount Sinai while receiving the commandments (Ex. 34:28), and Israel was in the wilderness 40 years (Deut. 8:2).

4:3 the tempter approached. The Spirit led Jesus into the wilderness but it is Satan who tests him. His challenges to Jesus come only after Jesus has entered a condition of physical weakness because of his fast. **If you are the Son of God.** This was a temptation to verify the truth of what God had declared (3:17). **bread.** Certainly it would be legitimate, Satan seemed to be saying, for God's own Son to do what God did when he supplied manna to the hungry Israelites. Jesus needed to be able to experience what we experience to bring us redemption (Heb. 4:15).

4:5 temple. The second temptation takes place at the temple, which is the focal point in Israel of God's love and power. The challenge is to prove this love and power of God by creating a peril from which God alone can rescue him.

4:6 If you are the Son of God. Once again the challenge is to demonstrate that Jesus is the Messiah. **it is written.** Satan now quotes Scripture, but does so in a way that tears it from its context. Psalm 91:11–12 are words of assurance to God's people that they can trust God to be with them even through difficult times. Satan twists this to mean that Jesus ought to deliberately put himself in a life-threatening situation to see if God really will bail him out.

4:9 I will give You all these things. Satan offers Jesus a painless, immediate way to power and fame. In fact, by his obedience to the Father, Jesus would become the King of kings, possessing all authority and power (Ps. 2:8; Dan. 7:14).

4:11 angels came and began to serve Him. One function of angels is to bring comfort and aid to God's people (Heb. 1:14). Thus prepared by his baptism and his temptation, Jesus begins his ministry.

SESSION 3 : JESUS' EARLY MINISTRY

SCRIPTURE LUKE 4:14-30

LAST WEEK

In last week's session, we focused on Jesus' baptism and temptation. We were encouraged by the fact that Jesus understands what we are going through when we struggle with temptation. We also talked about the need to give each other support and strength to help us live a life that is pleasing to God. Today we will consider the early part of Jesus' ministry and how many people had a difficult time accepting what he proclaimed.

ICE-BREAKER : CONNECT WITH YOUR GROUP | 15 MINUTES

LEADER: Choose one or two Ice-Breaker questions. If you have a new group member you may want to do all three to help him or her get acquainted. Remember to stick closely to the three-part agenda and the time allowed for each segment.

There's no place like home, be it ever so humble ... or dull, or exciting, or stressful or homey. Sometimes it's hard to be taken seriously by the very people who knew us when we were learning to walk. Take turns sharing what your hometown is like.

1. What do people say when you go back home, and why?

2. What is one of your fondest memories of your hometown?

3. How would you describe your hometown?
   - ☐ Laid-back.
   - ☐ Fast-paced.
   - ☐ Everybody knows everybody.
   - ☐ Small town.
   - ☐ Big city.
   - ☐ Other _____.

LEADER: Select two members of the group ahead of time to read aloud the Scripture passage. Then discuss the Questions for Interaction, dividing into subgroups of three to six.

Everyone has to start somewhere, and Jesus started in the region where he grew up. This passage records his first active ministry in his hometown of Nazareth. The response was not very good. Let's read Luke 4:14-30 and see what we can learn about Jesus' purpose on earth, and what our response should be.

Jesus Rejected at Nazareth

Reader One: ¹⁴Then Jesus returned to Galilee in the power of the Spirit, and news about Him spread throughout the entire vicinity. ¹⁵He was teaching in their synagogues, being acclaimed by everyone. ¹⁶He came to Nazareth, where He had been brought up. As usual, He entered the synagogue on the Sabbath day and stood up to read. ¹⁷The scroll of the prophet Isaiah was given to Him, and unrolling the scroll, He found the place where it was written:

Reader Two: ¹⁸"The Spirit of the Lord is upon Me,
because He has anointed Me
to preach good news to the poor.
He has sent Me to proclaim freedom to the captives
and recovery of sight to the blind,
to set free the oppressed,
¹⁹to proclaim the year of the Lord's favor."

Reader One: ²⁰He then rolled up the scroll, gave it back to the attendant, and sat down. And the eyes of everyone in the synagogue were fixed on Him. ²¹He began by saying to them, "Today this Scripture has been fulfilled in your hearing." ²²They were all speaking well of Him and were amazed by the gracious words that came from His mouth, yet they said, "Isn't this Joseph's son?"

Reader Two: ²³Then He said to them, "No doubt you will quote this proverb to Me: 'Doctor, heal yourself.' 'All we've heard that took place in Capernaum, do here in Your hometown also.' " ²⁴He also said, "I assure you: No prophet is accepted in his hometown. ²⁵But I say to you, there were certainly many widows in Israel in Elijah's days, when the sky was shut up for three years and six months while a great famine came over all the land. ²⁶Yet Elijah was not sent to any of them—but to a widow at Zarephath in Sidon. ²⁷And in the prophet Elisha's time, there were many in Israel who had serious skin diseases, yet not one of them was healed—but only Naaman the Syrian."

Reader One: ²⁸When they heard this, all who were in the synagogue were enraged. ²⁹They got up, drove Him out of town, and brought Him to the edge of the hill on which their town was built, intending to hurl Him over the cliff. ³⁰But He passed right through the crowd and went on His way.

Luke 4:14–30

QUESTIONS FOR INTERACTION

LEADER: Refer to the Summary and Study Notes at the end of this session as needed. If 30 minutes is not enough time to answer all of the questions in this section, conclude the Bible Study by answering question 7.

1. What was the status symbol for having "made it" in your hometown?

2. How do you think Jesus felt when he returned to his hometown? What did the remark about this being "Joseph's son" imply (v. 22)?

3. According to verses 18–19, what is Jesus' purpose on earth? What do these verses mean?

4. What did Jesus say to upset these people? Why did they go from amazement to anger so quickly?

5. What was Jesus' reaction to these people? How important are the phrases "the Spirit of the Lord is upon Me ... He has anointed Me," in helping him through that difficult interaction?

6. When have you been rejected? How did you react?

7. Which of these purposes of Jesus' ministry has meant the most to you recently, and why?
    - ❑ Preach good news to the poor.
    - ❑ Proclaim freedom to the captives.
    - ❑ Recovery of sight to the blind.
    - ❑ Set free the oppressed.
    - ❑ Proclaim the year of the Lord's favor.

8. What is the significance of the "year of the Lord" (v. 19)? How does it relate to us today?

CARING TIME : APPLY THE LESSON AND PRAY FOR ONE ANOTHER | 15 MIN.

LEADER: Begin the Caring Time by having group members take turns sharing responses to all three questions. Be sure to save at least the last five minutes for a time of group prayer. Remember to include a prayer for the empty chair when concluding the prayer time.

Encouraging and supporting each other is especially vital if this group is to become all it can be. Take time now to build up one another with sharing and prayer.

1. What is the best thing that happened to you last week? What is the worst?

2. When have you experienced rejection due to your faith? What helps you to stay strong in the face of rejection?

3. How can you continue to fulfill the ministry that you mentioned in question 7?

NEXT WEEK

Today we looked at the beginning of Jesus' earthly ministry. We saw how the people in his own hometown violently rejected him and his teachings. We were reminded how we will all face rejection at some point due to our faith, so we need to look to the Holy Spirit for help and strength. In the coming week, pray that the Holy Spirit will give you the boldness to share your faith with someone whom God has laid on your heart. Next week we will consider Jesus' calling of his first disciples, and see how their stories compare to our own.

Summary: Having affirmed his loyalty and faithfulness to God in a way that Israel has not been able to do, Jesus emerges from the wilderness empowered by God's Spirit. As this passage shows, the response to Jesus' ministry was mixed. On the one hand, Jesus ministry was highly popular with crowds. On the other hand, he was opposed by the people in his own hometown and the religious leaders.

4:14 Galilee. From 4:14–9:50, Luke records Jesus' ministry in Galilee, a province about 50 miles long and 25 miles wide in the north of Palestine. In the power of the Spirit. The Spirit led Jesus into his time of testing (4:1; Matt. 4:1), and the Spirit now empowers Jesus' ministry. Luke especially emphasizes the role of Jesus as the bearer of God's Spirit in fullness.

4:15 synagogues. While the temple in Jerusalem was the religious center for all Jews, the community synagogue was the focal point of weekly worship and teaching. Jesus' initial ministry was as a well-received itinerant preacher teaching in synagogues throughout Galilee. It is in the light of stories of his healings and teachings that he comes to his hometown of Nazareth.

4:16 Nazareth. Nazareth was located in a hollow surrounded by hills. **the Sabbath.** Each Sabbath, Jews would gather at the synagogue for a service of worship and instruction from the Scripture. There was a standard order governing which passages of the Law would be read, and the same may have been true about the reading from the Prophets as well. The synagogue had no formal clergy, so various men approved by the elders of the synagogue read and taught from the Scripture. Considering Jesus' emerging reputation, it is not surprising that he was asked to read and teach. **and stood up to read.** As a sign of reverence for God, men would stand as they read the Scripture, but sat down to teach.

4:17 The scroll. Since Nazareth was a small village, it is unlikely that the synagogue would have been able to afford to have scrolls of the entire sacred writings. The Isaiah scroll was undoubtedly a prized possession of the synagogue.

4:18 The passage Jesus read was from Isaiah 61:1–2 (with the addition of a phrase from 58:6). **The Spirit of the Lord is upon me.** The ministry of a prophet of God is one empowered by God's Spirit. **to preach good news/to proclaim freedom/recovery of sight.** When John the Baptist was in prison, wondering if Jesus is indeed the Messiah, Jesus sent back the message that the miraculous works are being performed: "the blind see, the lame walk ... good news is preached to the poor," (7:22; Matt. 11:4–5).The words that Jesus uses to comfort and assure John are from Isaiah 61:1 as well as 29:18–21 and 35:5–6. Because his hearers were well aware of the miracles he had already done, Jesus is stating, for those who can hear, that he is the Messiah. **set free the oppressed.** These words are not found in either the Hebrew or Greek versions of Isaiah 61, but are found in Isaiah 58:6. Certainly the infirmities that Jesus healed were oppressive, but even greater is the oppression of sin, and his greatest work was to set free the captives of sin.

4:19 the year of the Lord's favor. This refers to the Jubilee Year of Leviticus 25. Every 50 years, the Jews were to release their slaves, cancel all debts, and return land to the families of its original owners. While there is no record that the Jews ever kept that law, it became a symbol of the deliverance and new order of justice that God intended to bring about when he would right the wrongs suffered by his people (1:51–55).

4:21 Today this scripture has been fulfilled. The phrase is reminiscent of Mark 1:15, with its announcement that the "kingdom of God is near." In both cases, Jesus asserts that the new era foretold by Isaiah has begun because he has come to bring it about. Jesus' healings and exorcisms (which had made him so popular) were literal pointers to the truth that the new era of God's deliverance had begun and would come to pass through him. He is the one who truly does give sight. He is the one who actually has the power to set people free from tyranny. Jesus is clear about his claim: he is God's appointed Messiah (Matt. 11:4–6).

4:22 all speaking well of him. The violent response later in this story (v. 28) shows that the final reaction toward Jesus was decidedly negative. **amazed.** This word expresses bewilderment, perplexity, or astonishment, and can be used to show admiration or opposition. **Joseph's son.** In stark contrast to God's declaration in Luke 3:22 (Matt. 3:17) that Jesus is God's son, the hometown people could only see Jesus as Joseph's boy. Who did this carpenter's son think he was, anyway? The Messiah was supposed to come from Bethlehem (Mic. 5:2), not Nazareth.

4:23 Doctor, heal yourself. This proverb has both Greek and Arabic parallels. The doubt and cynicism of his hometown is seen in that they would not believe the stories they had heard elsewhere unless they could see further evidence. **Capernaum.** According to Mark's gospel, this is the village in which Jesus first began to teach and heal (Mark 1:21ff).

4:24 No prophet is accepted in his hometown. This proverb also has Greek parallels. It simply observes that typically the hardest place for a famous person to gain respect is among the people he or she grew up with. Jesus introduces it with "I tell you the truth," a phrase he uses when he wants his listeners to pay particular attention to what he is saying (12:37; 18:17,29; 21:32; 23:43). The irony is that while they will honor Isaiah as a prophet, they refuse to see the fulfillment of his word in Jesus.

4:25–27 While neither Elijah nor Elisha were rejected by their own people, their ministry extended to others outside of Israel as well. These stories, found in 1 Kings 17:1–18:2 and 2 Kings 5:1–27, illustrate that God has never limited his grace only to Israel. They further emphasize the point that if Nazareth (and, by extension, the Jews as a whole) will not receive Jesus with faith, then there are plenty of others who will.

4:28–29 Jesus' strong words, which implied that Gentiles were more worthy of God's grace than the people from Jesus' hometown, provoked such a strong response that a mob desired to kill him.

4:30 He passed right through the crowd. This illustrates the proper fulfillment of Psalm 91:11–12, which Satan had twisted in his temptation of Jesus (4:10–11).

SESSION 4 : JESUS CALLS HIS DISCIPLES

SCRIPTURE JOHN 1:35–51

LAST WEEK

Jesus' early ministry was our focus in last week's session. We saw how he was met with acceptance in Galilee, but with rejection in his hometown of Nazareth. We were reminded to depend on the power of the Holy Spirit to help us continue in our ministry, even in the face of rejection. Today we get a glimpse of the people Jesus called to be part of his small group and how they became his disciples.

ICE-BREAKER : CONNECT WITH YOUR GROUP | 15 MINUTES

LEADER: Welcome and introduce new group members. Choose one, two or all three of the Ice-Breaker questions.

When was the last time you thought about a career change? Sometimes opportunities will present themselves when we least expect it. The disciples certainly found that out when suddenly they were transformed from fishermen into Jesus' first followers. Take turns sharing your thoughts on your career dreams.

1. If you could choose another career field to work in, what would it be? Why?

2. If you were to open a new business, what would it be? Why?

3. Which of the following best describes you?
   - ☐ Responder to people.
   - ☐ Encourager of people.
   - ☐ Responder to a task.
   - ☐ Initiator of a task.

LEADER: Select two members of the group ahead of time to read aloud the Scripture passage. Then discuss the Questions for Interaction, dividing into subgroups of three to six.

Jesus called ordinary people to be in his inner circle. There was nothing special about them and, from the world's perspective, nothing special about Jesus. But these ordinary men turned the world upside down. Read John 1:35–51 and see how it all began.

Jesus Calls His Disciples

Reader One: [35]Again the next day, John was standing with two of his disciples. [36]When he saw Jesus passing by, he said, "Look! The Lamb of God!"

[37]The two disciples heard him say this and followed Jesus. [38]When Jesus turned and noticed them following Him, He asked them, "What are you looking for?"

They said to Him, "Rabbi" (which means "Teacher"), "where are You staying?"

[39]"Come and you'll see," He replied. So they went and saw where He was staying, and they stayed with Him that day. It was about 10 in the morning.

[40]Andrew, Simon Peter's brother, was one of the two who heard John and followed Him. [41]He first found his own brother Simon and told him, "We have found the Messiah!" (which means "Anointed One"), [42]and he brought Simon to Jesus.

When Jesus saw him, He said, "You are Simon, son of John. You will be called Cephas" (which means "Rock").

Reader Two: [43]The next day He decided to leave for Galilee. Jesus found Philip and told him, "Follow Me!"

[44]Now Philip was from Bethsaida, the hometown of Andrew and Peter. [45]Philip found Nathanael and told him, "We have found the One of whom Moses wrote in the law (and so did the prophets): Jesus the son of Joseph, from Nazareth!"

[46]"Can anything good come out of Nazareth?" Nathanael asked him.

"Come and see," Philip answered.

[47]Then Jesus saw Nathanael coming toward Him and said about him, "Here is a true Israelite in whom is no deceit."

[48]"How do you know me?" Nathanael asked.

"Before Philip called you, when you were under the fig tree, I saw you," Jesus answered.

[49]"Rabbi," Nathanael replied, "You are the Son of God! You are the King of Israel!"

⁵⁰Jesus responded to him, "Do you believe only because I told you I saw you under the fig tree? You will see greater things than this." ⁵¹Then He said, "I assure you: You will see heaven opened and the angels of God ascending and descending upon the Son of Man."

John 1:35–51

QUESTIONS FOR INTERACTION

LEADER:Refer to the Summary and Study Notes at the end of this session as needed. If 30 minutes is not enough time to answer all of the questions in this section, conclude the Bible Study by answering questions 6 and 7.

1. Who has been most influential in your life as a role model or teacher? What did you learn from this person?

2. Why do you think Jesus chose the men he did?

3. What did Andrew and Philip do once they heard that Jesus was the Messiah? What credentials did Philip use to convince Nathanael?

4. What is significant about changing the name of Simon to Cephas? At this point in the life of Cephas, was he "a rock"?

5. What was Jesus' promise to Philip and Nathanael in verse 51? What did it mean to them? What does it mean to you?

6. Which one of the following titles used to refer to Jesus in this passage means the most to you, and why?
  ☐ Lamb of God.
  ☐ Rabbi.
  ☐ Messiah.
  ☐ Son of God.
  ☐ King of Israel.
  ☐ Son of Man.

7. What is one way you can follow Jesus more closely in the coming week?

GOING DEEPER:

If your group has time and/or wants a challenge, go on to this question.

8. What do you think people are "looking for" today (v. 38)? How can you help them?

CARING TIME : APPLY THE LESSON AND PRAY FOR ONE ANOTHER | 15 MIN.

LEADER: Be sure to save at least 15 minutes for this important time. After sharing responses to all three questions and asking for prayer requests, close in a time of group prayer.

Being a follower of Christ means much more than just going to church on Sundays. It means learning to be a disciple, just as the Twelve had to learn what it meant to follow him. Take some time now to encourage one another in your faith by discussing the following questions and sharing prayer requests.

1. Who can you reach out to, like Andrew and Philip did, and invite to this group to learn about Jesus?

2. For what blessing in your life would you like to thank God today?

3. How can the group pray for you as you endeavor to follow Jesus more closely in the coming week (see question 7)?

NEXT WEEK

Today we saw Jesus call his first disciples. We considered how Jesus chose ordinary men and women to help him accomplish his ministry on earth, and that he continues to use ordinary men and women today. In the coming week, follow through on inviting to the group the person you mentioned in question 1 during the Caring Time, and trust Jesus to work through you. Next week we will look at Jesus' interaction with the religious people of the synagogues.

Summary: Jesus did not conduct his ministry all alone. He called 12 men to be his close companions. Many others also became his disciples, including women. The identity of Jesus is progressively revealed through the series of titles. He is called the Lamb of God, Rabbi, Messiah, the Son of God, the King of Israel and the Son of Man. The author's intention here is not so much to give a chronological account of Jesus' first days of ministry but clearly to declare Jesus' identity to his readers right from the beginning.

1:35 John. This refers to John the Baptist, who was baptizing "at Bethany on the other side of the Jordan" (1:28). **two of his disciples.** A disciple was simply a person who adhered to the teachings of a particular rabbi or inspired teacher. John the Baptist had enormous popular appeal, and had gathered many disciples, at least one from as far away as Alexandria in Egypt who went to Ephesus in present-day Turkey (Acts 18:24-19:3).

1:38 What are you looking for? The motivation of those who would follow him is a concern for Jesus (2:24; 6:26). Discipleship requires a person to declare clearly his or her intentions. **Rabbi.** Rabbis were teachers who gathered disciples around them. This is the recognition of Jesus' teaching authority. **staying.** This is the same word translated in verse 33 as "remain." As such, it hints that the concern in this question ("Where are you staying?") is on Jesus' true dwelling place. In this Gospel, recognition of Jesus' identity is tied up with recognizing where he is from and where he is going (8:21; 9:30; 14:2-6).

1:39 Come and you'll see. On the one hand, this appears to be a simple invitation to accompany Jesus to his residence. On the other hand, by this statement Jesus invites these followers to enter into the journey of discipleship with him. Only as they commit themselves to follow him will they perceive the nature of his true home and identity. **ten.** Literally about the 10th hour. At that time there were various methods of determining time. John most likely used a different method than the other Gospels. If the method of the other Gospel is used it would have been about 4 P.M.

1:41 We have found the Messiah. This is another title the author uses to identify Jesus. The Messiah was the one the people of Israel expected would be sent from God to deliver them from their oppression by Rome and restore Israel to its former greatness as a nation. He would be like the ancient King David, a powerful king who would rally his people together in a fight for freedom. Jesus poured a new meaning into this word. He taught that the deliverance he came to bring was a deliverance from sin that would usher in the kingdom of God. **Anointed One.** This parenthetical expression is the author's commentary to his readers as he translates the Hebrew term "Messiah" into its Greek equivalent "Christ."

1:42 Cephas. The Aramaic name Cephas and the Greek name Peter both mean "rock." Although Peter sometimes seemed both inconsistent and uncertain during Jesus' time with him (18:15-17,25-27), Peter became the chief spokesman for the apostles after Jesus returned to heaven and the Holy Spirit came at Pentecost (Acts 2:14). The implication is that the decision to come to Jesus is one that will change a person from the inside out, producing a new character.

1:43 Galilee. So far the story has centered in Judea. Galilee, where Jesus spent his boyhood, was a province 60 miles north of Jerusalem. One of the reasons the Pharisees rejected Jesus' claim to messiahship was because they assumed he was born in Galilee. On the basis of Micah 5:2, they expected the Christ to be born in Bethlehem (7:41,52).

1:44 Bethsaida. This was a village on the Sea of Galilee.

1:45 Nathanael. Like Andrew, Philip's response to discovering Jesus was to tell someone else. While Philip is found in the list of apostles mentioned in the other Gospels, Nathanael is not. It may be that he also bore the name Bartholomew, since in the other Gospels Philip and Bartholomew are mentioned together (Mark 3:18). It is also possible that he may not have been one of the apostles at all. **Moses wrote in the law.** This refers to the Prophet to come (Deut. 18:18), the fulfillment of the Old Testament hope. **and so did the prophets.** This refers to the common Old Testament expectation that God would send a leader who would save his people (Isa. 11:1–9; Mic. 5:2).

1:46 Nazareth! This was a small, insignificant village in Galilee. It seemed impossible to Nathanael that the one Philip described could come from such a place.

1:47 a true Israelite. Jesus' greeting implies an awareness of Nathanael's spiritual motivations reflected in that Nathanael, unlike Israel as a whole, came to Jesus with sincerity. Israel was to be a people prepared to respond to God, but for the most part the nation failed to reflect that purpose. **in whom is no deceit.** This was not flattery, nor blindness to the fact that Nathanael had faults. Rather, it's a statement affirming Nathanael's sincerity and openness to God. He is an example of someone "pure in heart" (Matt. 5:8) in that, unlike so many others (1:11), he truly seeks to know and follow God.

1:48 I saw you. This accents the supernatural knowledge of Jesus.

1:49 Son of God! John refers to Jesus as God's Son in 1:14,18, and in the most well known passage, 3:16. Jesus, as Creator, always was, from the very beginning, but as Psalm 2:7 says, (Heb. 1), "You are my son, today I have become your Father."

1:50 greater things. This is probably an allusion to the miracles Jesus will perform as signs of his divine identity, culminated by the grand miracle of his resurrection.

1:51 you. This is a plural term referring to all who believe, not just Nathanael. **the Son of Man.** Of all the titles for Jesus in this chapter, this is the one he uses for himself. Daniel 7:13ff provides its background as the one invested with divine authority to rule the earth, but it was not a commonly used term for the Messiah in Jesus' time. He may have used it precisely because it did not invoke the narrowly nationalistic stereotypes of the Messiah.

SESSION 5 : JESUS AND THE RELIGIOUS LEADERS

SCRIPTURE MARK 2:13–22; 3:1–6

LAST WEEK

In last week's session, we saw how Jesus called ordinary men to be his disciples. We were reminded that God can use us in the same way to carry the Gospel to others—we only need to depend upon the Holy Spirit and each other for help and guidance. Today we are going to see how Jesus interacted with the religious leaders of his day, and consider how religious rules and regulations can stand in the way of our relationship with Jesus.

ICE-BREAKER : CONNECT WITH YOUR GROUP | 15 MINUTES

LEADER: Open with a word of prayer, and then introduce any new people or visitors. To help new group members get acquainted, remember to do all three Ice-Breaker questions.

Once upon a time everything was closed on Sundays because it was assumed in America that people went to church and spent time as a family on the Lord's Day. But then again, once upon a time taxes were low and bread was cheap! Take turns sharing your thoughts and experiences with change in your life.

1. What church traditions do you no longer follow that your parents followed?

2. Growing up, what was something you weren't allowed to do on Sunday?

3. Who did you like to hang around with in high school? Who do you still keep in contact with from those days?

LEADER: Select three members of the group ahead of time to read aloud the Scripture passage. Divide the readings as outlined. Then discuss the Questions for Interaction, dividing into subgroups of three to six.

The religious leaders of Jesus' day had a list of "do's and don'ts" to which they expected people to adhere. These lists had nothing to do with being spiritual or following God. Jesus had a way of upsetting the religious leaders when he did things to challenge their "lists." Let's read Mark 2:13–22; 3:1–6 and see where we fit in this story–as a religious person caught up in certain lists or as a follower who will do whatever it takes to bring lost people to Jesus.

Jesus and the Religious Leaders

Reader One: [13]Then Jesus went out again beside the sea. The whole crowd was coming to Him, and He taught them. [14]Then, moving on, He saw Levi the son of Alphaeus sitting at the tax office, and He said to him, "Follow Me!" So he got up and followed Him.

[15]While He was reclining at the table in Levi's house, many tax collectors and sinners were also guests with Jesus and His disciples, because there were many who were following Him. [16]When the scribes of the Pharisees saw that He was eating with sinners and tax collectors, they asked His disciples, "Why does He eat with tax collectors and sinners?"

[17]When Jesus heard this, He told them, "Those who are well don't need a doctor, but the sick do need one. I didn't come to call the righteous, but sinners."

Reader Two: [18]Now John's disciples and the Pharisees were fasting. People came and asked Him, "Why do John's disciples and the Pharisees' disciples fast, but Your disciples do not fast?"

[19]Jesus said to them, "The wedding guests cannot fast while the groom is with them, can they? As long as they have the groom with them, they cannot fast. [20]But the time will come when the groom is taken away from them, and then they will fast in that day. [21]No one sews a patch of unshrunk cloth on an old garment. Otherwise, the new patch pulls away from the old cloth, and a worse tear is made. [22]And no one puts new wine into old wineskins. Otherwise, the wine will burst the skins, and the wine is lost as well as the skins. But new wine is for fresh wineskins."

Reader Three: **3** [1]Now He entered the synagogue again, and a man was there who had a paralyzed hand. [2]In order to accuse Him, they were watching Him closely to see whether He would heal him on the Sabbath. [3]He told the man with the paralyzed hand, "Stand before us." ⁴Then He said to them, "Is it lawful on the Sabbath to do good or to do evil, to save life or to kill?" But they were silent. ⁵After looking around at them with anger and sorrow at the hardness of their hearts, He told the man, "Stretch out your hand." So he stretched it out, and his hand was restored. ⁶Immediately the Pharisees went out and started plotting with the Herodians against Him, how they might destroy Him.

Mark 2:13-22; 3:1-6

QUESTIONS FOR INTERACTION

LEADER:Refer to the Summary and Study Notes at the end of this session as needed. If 30 minutes is not enough time to answer all of the questions in this section, conclude the Bible Study by answering question 7.

1. When you were growing up, with what people were you told not to associate, and why?
   - ☐ People of another faith or denomination.
   - ☐ Public school kids.
   - ☐ Those who were poor.
   - ☐ Kids who lived on the wrong side of town.
   - ☐ Other _____.

2. Why did Jesus "hang out" at a party with a bunch of sinners? What did the religious people think he had become (Matt. 11:19)?

3. Why were the people concerned that Jesus' disciples weren't fasting? What was Jesus' explanation?

4. Why did the religious leaders want to kill Jesus after he healed the man in the synagogue? Who would you say are like these religious leaders today?

5. Why is there a stigma among some in the Christian community about other Christians who want to hang out with lost people (whether it is at a bar, a dance club, concert, etc.) simply to build a relationship with them and win them to Christ?

6. Do you have an ongoing friendship with any lost people? What "extreme" thing would you do to build a relationship with a lost friend or neighbor?

7. What religious rules are you still holding on to with the belief that they demonstrate your spirituality?

If your group has time and/or wants a challenge, go on to this question.

8. What do the illustrations of the garments and wineskins mean for the church today?

CARING TIME : APPLY THE LESSON AND PRAY FOR ONE ANOTHER | 15 MIN.

LEADER: Encourage everyone to participate in this important time and be sure that each group member is receiving prayer support. Continue to pray for the empty chair in the closing group prayer.

Comfort and encourage one another with this time of sharing and prayer. Begin by sharing your responses to the following questions. Be sure to offer any other prayer requests and concerns before closing in prayer.

1. If you were to hang around with unbelievers, would they recognize any difference between you and themselves? What would the differences be?

2. Who would you like to see come to Christ? What steps will you need to take so you can be used of God to see that happen?

3. How can we pray for you regarding the religious rules you are still holding on to (question 7)?

NEXT WEEK

Today we looked at Jesus' interaction with the religious people of the synagogues. We saw how upset they got with Jesus when he put people's needs before their rules and regulations. We also considered how we may be doing the same thing, and in the process not being open to spending time with non-Christians. Take some time this week to pray and ask God if there is someone with whom you should develop a relationship to help this person along on the spiritual journey. Next week we will look at the healing ministry of Jesus.

Summary: In session 3, we encountered the beginning of opposition to the ministry of Jesus. The reactions against him in Nazareth were unusual, however, since most of the people were quite enthusiastic about Jesus. His real opposition came from the religious leaders. In the three stories in today's passage, we see them probe Jesus, question him and then come to the awful conclusion that not only is Jesus dangerous, he needs to be killed.

2:14 Levi. Elsewhere Levi is identified as Matthew (Matt. 9:9), the disciple who eventually wrote one of the Gospels. In his role as a tax collector, Matthew would have been hated by both the religious establishment and the common people. For Jesus to associate with Levi and his friends would raise the same objections most church people today would feel if they knew their pastor was associating closely with anyone extorting money from people. **Follow me.** In Matthew, Mark and Luke, this is the key phrase regarding discipleship. Only those who leave their past behind to follow Jesus in faith and obedience are his disciples.

2:15 reclining at the table. To share a meal with another was a significant event, implying acceptance of that person. In this way, Jesus extends his "friendship" to those who were outside orthodox religious life. **"sinners."** This would include the overtly evil (robbers, prostitutes, murderers, liars and yes, tax collectors, as well as those who did not keep the Mosaic law.

2:16 Pharisees. This was a small, strict sect of Jews who devoted themselves to observing the traditions of the rabbis as a means of gaining God's favor. Seeing themselves as the truly righteous in Israel, they tended as a whole to look down upon other Jews who could not follow their practices. **Why does he eat.** They could not understand how a truly religious person could eat with rabble who might serve food not prepared according to ritual, on dishes that were ritually (though not literally) unclean.

2:18 John's disciples. These are the followers of John the Baptist. **the Pharisees.** Members of a small (about 6,000 members at the time of Herod) but powerful religious sect whose prime concern was knowing and keeping the Old Testament Law in all its detail. **fasting.** Although the Old Testament Law did not require it, the Pharisees did not eat from 6 A.M. to 6 P.M. on Mondays and Thursdays as an act of piety. Regular fasting was assumed to be part of any serious religious discipline. The implication of the question is that there is something deficient about Jesus' disciples, because they do not observe rituals of fasting.

2:19 groom. In the Old Testament, God was often referred to as Israel's groom, another subtle indication of Jesus' divine identity.

2:20 is taken away from them. An ominous note predicting Jesus' death. That would be an appropriate time for fasting as a genuine expression of his disciples' grief for sin and desire for God's mercy.

2:22 new wine. New wine is still fermenting. Hence, no one would have poured it into a leather container which was old, dry and crusty. New wine required new skins which were supple and flexible, able to expand as the wine fermented. Otherwise, the fermenting wine would burst the skin, ruining the skin and spilling the wine.

33:2 they were watching Him closely. By this time the religious leaders no longer

41

questioned Jesus. Now they simply watched to see if his actions betrayed a disregard for the Law so they might accuse him. **whether He would heal him on the Sabbath.** The issue is not healing, but whether Jesus would do so on the Sabbath in defiance of the oral tradition, which allowed healing only if there was danger to life. Jesus could have waited until the next day to heal this long-paralyzed hand. These Pharisees fail to see the need of the man, focusing only on the mandates of their tradition.

3:3 Stand before us. As with the paralytic (2:1–12), Jesus once again takes a deliberate action to force the confrontation with his questioners. He did not shy away from their accusations, but took action to expose the foolishness of the charges of his opponents.

3:4 He said to them. Jesus began this series of confrontations with a question (2:8–9) and ends it with another. The religious leaders may have been investigating Jesus, but Jesus was also getting to know their hearts. Jesus' implication is that refusing to heal this man just because it was the Sabbath was actually to commit evil, since a real human need would be allowed to go unmet. **they were silent.** Their silence reflected their refusal to reconsider their position.

3:5 anger/sorrow. Jesus felt strongly about the injustice of a system that sacrificed the genuine needs of people for religious traditions that had nothing to do with God. **hardness of their hearts.** Just as the religious leaders have come to a conclusion about him (3:6), he has come to understand them. Their problem is that their hearts (the center of their beings) have calcified. The Greek word translated "stubborn" is also used to describe a gall stone or a tooth. Later Jesus will indicate that the disciples have the same problem (6:52; 8:17). **Stretch out your hand.** Just as he deliberately declared the paralytic's sins forgiven (2:1–12), he deliberately heals on the Sabbath, knowing that this was blasphemy to the teachers of the Law.

3:6 Herodians. A political group made up of influential Jewish sympathizers of King Herod. They were normally despised by the Pharisees, who considered them traitors (for working with Rome) and irreligious (unclean as a result of their association with Gentiles). However, the Pharisees had no power to kill Jesus. Only the civil authority can do this, and hence the collaboration. **how they might destroy Him.** Mark makes use of irony here. The Pharisees believed Jesus violated the Sabbath by healing on that day, but failed to see that they themselves were violating the Law by plotting how to kill him on that day!

SESSION 6 : JESUS HEALS

SCRIPTURE MATTHEW 9:18-34

LAST WEEK

In last week's session, we looked at Jesus' interaction with the religious leaders and how angry they got when Jesus didn't follow all of their rules and regulations. Jesus reminded us that reaching out to people and meeting their needs should always come before religious piety. Today we will observe Jesus' power to heal physical infirmities and the soul.

ICE-BREAKER : CONNECT WITH YOUR GROUP | 15 MINUTES

LEADER: Choose one or two of the Ice-Breaker questions. If you have a new group member, you may want to do all three. Remember to stick closely to the three-part agenda and the time allowed for each segment.

Nobody likes being sick, though some of us make better patients than others. Some of us also make better caregivers than others! Take turns sharing your own thoughts and experiences regarding illness or caring for someone else.

1. What is the sickest you have ever been? What did you do to get well? What role did a doctor play in your getting better?

2. Do you believe God can still heal today? Why or why not?

3. Do you know anyone who has been in a coma and come out of it? What was that experience like? Did they recall anything unusual?

It's hard to imagine what it would have been like to be on earth when Jesus was walking on it and healing people. What a special time to live. And, most importantly, he touched people spiritually, as well as physically. Let's read Matthew 9:18–34 and learn how Jesus can heal our souls.

LEADER: Select two members of the group ahead of time to read aloud the Scripture passage. Have one member read verses 18–26, and the other read verses 27–34. Then discuss the Questions for Interaction, dividing into subgroups of three to six.

Jesus Heals

Reader One: ¹⁸As He was telling them these things, suddenly one of the leaders came and knelt down before Him, saying, "My daughter is near death, but come and lay Your hand on her, and she will live." ¹⁹So Jesus and His disciples got up and followed him.

²⁰Just then, a woman who had suffered from bleeding for 12 years approached from behind and touched the tassel on His robe, ²¹for she said to herself, "If I can just touch His robe, I'll be made well!"

²²But Jesus turned and saw her. "Have courage, daughter," He said. "Your faith has made you well." And the woman was made well from that moment.

²³When Jesus came to the leader's house, He saw the flute players and a crowd lamenting loudly. ²⁴"Leave," He said, "because the girl isn't dead, but sleeping." And they started laughing at Him. ²⁵But when the crowd had been put outside, He went in and took her by the hand, and the girl got up. ²⁶And this news spread throughout that whole area.

Reader Two: ²⁷As Jesus went on from there, two blind men followed Him, shouting, "Have mercy on us, Son of David!"

²⁸When He entered the house, the blind men approached Him, and Jesus said to them, "Do you believe that I can do this?"

"Yes, Lord," they answered Him.

²⁹Then He touched their eyes, saying, "Let it be done for you according to your faith!" ³⁰And their eyes were opened. Then Jesus warned them sternly, "Be sure that no one finds out!" ³¹But they went out and spread the news about Him throughout that whole area.

³²Just as they were going out, a demon-possessed man who was unable to speak was brought to Him. ³³When the demon had been driven out, the man spoke. And the crowds were amazed, saying, "Nothing like this has ever been seen in Israel!"

³⁴The Pharisees however, said, "He drives out demons by the ruler of the demons!"

Matthew 9:18–34

QUESTIONS FOR INTERACTION

LEADER: Refer to the Summary and Study Notes at the end of this session as needed. If 30 minutes is not enough time to answer all of the questions in this section, conclude the Bible Study by answering questions 6 and 7.

1. Do you have a hard time asking for help? Why or why not?

2. Who was this leader that humbled himself before Jesus? Why was this significant?

3. What did the ruler, the sick woman and the blind men have in common in asking Jesus to heal them? How important is this to one's healing?

4. What did the blind men believe about Jesus by calling him the Son of David (v. 27)? Why did Jesus not want them to tell anyone?

5. When Jesus casts out a demon (vv. 33–34), what is the reaction of: the crowd, the Pharisees and you?

6. In what area of your life are you struggling with faith?
   - ❏ Physical.
   - ❏ Social.
   - ❏ Spiritual.
   - ❏ Emotional.
   - ❏ Other _____.

7. What does Jesus need to restore in your life?
   - ❏ My relationship with him.
   - ❏ My relationship with someone else.
   - ❏ Health.
   - ❏ Finances.
   - ❏ Job.
   - ❏ Ministry.
   - ❏ Other _____.

GOING DEEPER: If your group has time and/or wants a challenge, go on to this question.

8. In the four miracles from this passage, what is it that Jesus restores? What does this tell you about Jesus?

LEADER: Be sure to save at least 15 minutes for this time of prayer and encouragement. Continue to encourage group members to invite new people to the group. Remind them that this group is for learning and sharing, but also for reaching out to others.

One of the central purposes of this group is to care for one another, even during times of suffering or sickness. Spend some time learning how the group can look after others who are in need of some care.

1. How is your relationship with Jesus right now?
   - ❏ Close.
   - ❏ Distant.
   - ❏ Improving.
   - ❏ Strained.
   - ❏ Other _____.

2. Is there anyone you know that we can pray for who needs a healing touch from Jesus?

3. How can the group pray for the restoration you need in your life (question 7)?

NEXT WEEK

Today we focused on the healing ministry of Jesus for the physical and spiritual needs of people. We saw how important faith is to being healed and how Jesus did not want healing to distract from his ultimate goal of saving souls. In the coming week, pray that God would give you the kind of faith that will bring healing to your life and the lives of those you touch. Next week we will look at Jesus teaching the disciples about his ultimate purpose as the Messiah.

Summary: Opposition or not, Jesus' ministry flourished. While the leaders railed at him for not being religiously orthodox, Jesus simply went about healing people. The four miracles in this passage show Jesus restoring health, life, sight and speech. As with the other miracles these are not simply meant to impress Matthew's readers with Jesus' power. They are meant to be pointers to Jesus' identity as the Servant of God who has come to establish the new order of God's kingdom (Isa. 61:1–3). The very nature of the healings provides insights regarding what the kingdom of God will be like when it is fully revealed. It is a realm of restoration and life. In God's kingdom there is freedom from all types of forces that oppress and destroy. It is a realm inaugurated by Jesus the Messiah. The first three stories stress the importance of faith in Jesus as the means of entering into the goodness of God's realm. The final story reveals the crisis of decision that Jesus produces: while some are amazed and proclaim his praises, others slander and insult him as the Devil himself.

9:18 one of the Leaders. Mark and Luke indicate that this man was the ruler of the local synagogue. In first-century Israel, the temple in Jerusalem was the sole place for sacrifice and was attended by numerous priests and other officials. In contrast, synagogues were found in each city and town where people met weekly on the Sabbath for worship and instruction. Synagogues were run by a committee of lay people (the rulers) who were responsible for the care of the building and for arranging services. **knelt down before Him.** In contrast to the skepticism and criticism of the religious authorities in the passages just prior to this story, this man comes with reverence and respect for Jesus. In light of the opposition Jesus has received from the official leaders of the people, it could not have been easy for this man, a leader in his community, to humble himself before Jesus in this way. But his concern for his daughter outweighed his pride. **lay Your hand on her.** The laying on of hands was a common practice for ordination, for blessing and for healing.

9:20 a woman who had suffered from bleeding. This woman was probably hemorrhaging from the womb. In addition to the obvious physical weakness such a chronic problem would produce, this particular problem rendered her ritually impure or unclean (Lev. 15:25–30). As a result, she was not allowed to take part in temple worship, was unable to have any sexual relations with her husband, and was not supposed to be present in a crowd where others might brush up against her and also become "unclean." The long-term effects of this stigma must have eroded her marriage, her self-concept and her relationship with God.

9:21 touch His robe. Somehow, this woman had heard of Jesus' power and took the chance that he might heal her. Perhaps out of fear of rejection because she was "unclean," she did not even dare approach Jesus openly like the ruler. She simply wanted to touch his robe without drawing any attention to herself at all. In a quasi-magical way, the power of a person was thought to be transferred to his or her clothing. The ruler thought that his daughter could be healed by Jesus' touch (v. 14). This woman thought she could be healed by touching his clothing.

9:22 Have courage, daughter. Jesus not only had power to heal her body; his words are intended to heal her spirit as he affirms her as a true child of God. **Your faith has made you well.** It was her faith that impelled her to reach out to Jesus—the source of healing power. Jesus' words point out that there is no magic involved in his healing. It is a matter of God's response to her faith in reaching out to him. The word Jesus uses to tell her that she is healed comes from the same root as the words "salvation" and "Savior." Spiritual as well as physical healing is in view here. As in other times in his ministry, Jesus shows that he is not afraid of being made "unclean" by the touch of the needy and sinners.

9:23 flute players and a crowd lamenting loudly. These were in all likelihood professional mourners. Even the poorest person was required to hire not less than two flutes and one wailing woman to mourn a death.

9:24 the girl isn't dead, but sleeping. Jesus does not mean by this that she has not really died but instead is in some sort of coma. The presence of the mourners and the laughter that greeted this statement all say the same thing: the child was truly dead. Jesus uses this same expression in reference to Lazarus, and he was clearly dead. His body had even begun to decompose (John 11:11–15). What he means is that she is not permanently dead.

9:25 the girl got up. Jesus raises her from the dead.

9:27 two blind men. Blindness was common in the ancient world, often due to infection. Blindness was of various sorts. The most widespread condition was ophthalmia, a form of conjunctivitis that was highly contagious. It was transmitted by flies and was aggravated by the dust and glare of the arid Middle Eastern environment. Blindness also resulted from glaucoma and cataracts, and was sometimes present at birth. **Have mercy on us.** Mercy is not as much an emotion as it is concrete aid. **Son of David.** There was a strong expectation that the Messiah would be a king in the line of David. The Messiah was understood to have the power to heal (11:4–5). Three of the four times in Matthew where there is an appeal for mercy, the title Son of David is used.

9:29 according to your faith. As with the story of the woman (v. 22), faith in Christ is shown to be the key that provides access to God's gracious power. The point is that God delights to respond to those who place their hope in him. But God is not a genie, nor is faith the magic lamp that gets God to do what one wants. True faith is not denial of fear or positive thinking; it is a gift from God that gives us sure hope of his loving care for us (Eph. 2:8).

9:33 Nothing like this has ever been seen in Israel! At the end of the Sermon on the Mount, Matthew contrasted Jesus' teaching with that of the religious leaders (7:28–29). Here he contrasts his healing power with theirs. In terms of both teaching and healing Jesus stands above and against the religious leaders.

SESSION 7 : JESUS THE MESSIAH

SCRIPTURE MARK 8:27–38

LAST WEEK

Jesus' healing ministry was our focus in last week's session. We considered how important faith is in the healing process, and saw how Jesus' ultimate concern was always the health of a person's soul. Today we will hear Jesus declare very clearly to his disciples his ultimate purpose as the Messiah.

ICE-BREAKER : CONNECT WITH YOUR GROUP | 15 MINUTES

LEADER: Open with a word of prayer, and then introduce and welcome any new group members. Choose one, two or all three Ice-Breaker questions to get started.

Everyone has some character traits that are wonderful and beautiful. We are, after all, made in God's image. But sometimes we can feel that our best qualities are overlooked by the people around us, and we may in turn miss the true value of some of our closest friends. Take turns sharing some thoughts about character traits.

1. What two qualities would you like people to see in you, and why?

2. What two qualities do you look for in a good friend, and why?

3. How do you react when someone says something you don't want to hear?

LEADER: Select a member of the group ahead of time to read aloud the Scripture passage. Then discuss the Questions for Interaction, dividing into subgroups of three to six.

Jesus' ultimate purpose in being here was to die on the cross for the sins of the world. The disciples did not fully understand that or what it meant to be a follower of Jesus. Let's read Mark 8:27–38 and see what it means to follow Jesus completely.

Jesus the Messiah

[27]Jesus went out with His disciples to the villages of Caesarea Philippi. And on the road He asked His disciples, "Who do people say that I am?"

[28]And they answered Him, "John the Baptist; others, Elijah; still others, one of the prophets."

[29]"But you," He asked them again, "who do you say that I am?"

Peter answered Him, "You are the Messiah!"

[30]And He strictly warned them to tell no one about Him.

[31]Then He began to teach them that the Son of Man must suffer many things, and be rejected by the elders, the chief priests, and the scribes, be killed, and rise after three days. [32]And He was openly talking about this. So Peter took Him aside and began to rebuke Him.

[33]But turning around and looking at His disciples, He rebuked Peter and said, "Get behind Me, Satan, because you're not thinking about God's concerns, but man's!"

[34]Summoning the crowd along with His disciples, He said to them, "If anyone wants to be My follower, he must deny himself, take up his cross, and follow Me. [35]For whoever wants to save his life will lose it, but whoever loses his life because of Me and the gospel will save it. [36]For what does it benefit a man to gain the whole world yet lose his life? [37]What can a man give in exchange for his life? [38]For whoever is ashamed of Me and of My words in this adulterous and sinful generation, the Son of Man will also be ashamed of him when He comes in the glory of His Father with the holy angels."

Mark 8:27–38

QUESTIONS FOR INTERACTION

LEADER: Refer to the Summary and Study Notes at the end of this session as needed. If 30 minutes is not enough time to answer all of the questions in this section, conclude the Bible Study by answering questions 6 and 7.

1 What word best describes how you feel about Jesus right now, and why?
   - ❏ Kind.
   - ❏ Compassionate.
   - ❏ Forgiving.
   - ❏ Convicting.
   - ❏ Silent.
   - ❏ Other _____.

2. Who did the people of Jesus' day think he was (v. 28)? Why would they associate him with these men?

3. Why did Jesus tell the disciples not to tell anyone his true identity? What was he concerned about?

4. Why did Peter rebuke Jesus? What were he and the others expecting out of Jesus, their Messiah?

5. What does Jesus say about Peter's thinking? If you had been Peter, how would you have felt? Think about how you would feel if you knew that someone you love dearly and admire deeply had only a few more weeks to live.

6. According to verses 34–38, what is involved in being a follower of Christ?

7. Of the commands that Jesus makes in verses 34–38, which one is hardest for you to follow, and why? Which one is easiest, and why?
   - ❏ Denying myself.
   - ❏ Taking up my cross.
   - ❏ Following Jesus in all areas of my life.
   - ❏ Detaching myself from the world and all it offers.
   - ❏ Not being ashamed and timid about my faith.
   - ❏ Other _____.

GOING DEEPER: If your group has time and/or wants a challenge, go on to this question.

8. While many Christians today are being persecuted for Christ in other countries, the residents of North America have not had to face this. Do you think we will face it? How do you feel about that?

LEADER: Continue to encourage group members to invite new people to the group. Close the group prayer by thanking God for each member and for this time together.

Some of Jesus' teachings were hard for his listeners to understand and accept, and they are just as hard today. He warns us that following him will require us to "take up our cross" daily. Take some time now to help and encourage one another to carry those personal crosses.

1. How are you doing as a follower of Christ?
   - ❒ I'm struggling right now.
   - ❒ I feel pretty good about where I am.
   - ❒ I want to know him more.
   - ❒ This is the richest time of my life.
   - ❒ Other _____.

2. What "cross" are you carrying that you would like the group to pray about?

3. How can the group pray for you regarding the command that is difficult for you to follow, as mentioned in question 7?

NEXT WEEK

Today we saw the disciples understand that Jesus is the Messiah, but misunderstand his purpose as the Messiah. We considered how Jesus' ultimate purpose was to suffer and die for the sins of the world. We were also reminded of what it truly means to be a follower of Christ. In the coming week, take some time to evaluate your life and see if you are following Christ in all areas. Ask for the Holy Spirit's wisdom and guidance. Next week we will look at the transfiguration of Jesus and consider its importance for the disciples who witnessed it, as well as for all of Christianity.

Summary: This is a pivotal passage in the Gospel of Mark. The disciples declare (through Peter, who seems to have become their spokesman) that in contrast to the crowds, they recognize who Jesus is. He is the long-expected Messiah. To be sure, they have the wrong idea about the nature and role of the Messiah. But at least they have grasped accurately that Jesus is not just an exceptional rabbi, nor just a wonder-worker.

8:27 Caesarea Philippi. A beautiful city near the slopes of Mount Hermon, 25 miles north of Bethsaida. It had been a center of Baal worship, and was said to be the birthplace of the god Pan. It was also the place where the River Jordan began. At the time when Jesus and his disciples visited there, up on the hill was a gleaming, white marble temple dedicated to the worship of Caesar. It was in this notably pagan region that Jesus asks his disciples if they understand that he is the Anointed One sent by God.

8:29 who do you say I am? This is the crucial question in Mark's gospel. By it the author forces his readers to consider how they will answer the question as well. **You are the Messiah!** Peter correctly identifies him as the Messiah. In the context of Jewish thought, this meant the prophesied future king of Israel who would deliver Israel from bondage into an era of freedom, power, influence and prosperity.

8:30 to tell no one. Jesus urges them to be silent about what they know. The problem is that although they know that he is the Messiah, they do not yet know what kind of Messiah he is. This recognition of Jesus follows immediately after the strange two-stage healing of the blind man (8:22–26) that one can parallel with the disciples' insight. Like the blind man, the disciples have received the "first touch" of healing. Their spiritual blindness, which thus far prevented them from understanding Jesus, is beginning to be healed but they are not yet totally restored to full sight as the next incident shows (8:31–33). After the heady, demanding days of miracles, teaching and healing the crowds, days which encouraged the disciples to think of an emerging earthly kingdom, Jesus takes the disciples to this remote area to prepare them for the coming events of the triumphal entry into Jerusalem and the seeming defeat of the crucifixion.

8:31 To predict one's death is rare, but not unknown. However, to predict that one will rise from the dead is startling. No wonder the disciples had trouble taking in what he was saying. The repetition three times of this prediction of death and resurrection draws attention to its central importance in understanding who Jesus is. **Then He began to teach them.** For the remainder of this unit (8:31–10:52), Jesus seeks to teach the Twelve what kind of Messiah he is. They think of him in popular terms: as a military hero who will lead a literal army in battle against the Romans from which he will emerge triumphant and be crowned king. **Son of Man.** This is the title that Jesus prefers for himself. In the first century it was a rather colorless, indeterminate title (with some messianic overtones) which could be translated as "man" or even "I." This allows Jesus to fill it with new meaning and to convey what kind of Messiah he actually is. **rejected by the elders, chief priests, and the scribes.** These three groups made up the Sanhedrin, the ruling Jewish body. Jesus is predicting that he will be officially rejected by Israel (14:55). **be killed.** The death of the Messiah at the hands of Israel's official governing body played no part in popular ideas about

53

the Messiah. This was a startling, incomprehensible announcement. For Jesus, his death was mandated by a divine necessity.

8:32 rebuke. Peter, who moments before identifies Jesus as the Messiah, is startled by his teaching that the Messiah will suffer, be rejected, killed and then rise from the dead. He felt compelled to take Jesus aside and urge him to stop this line of teaching. The word "rebuke" is the same one used to describe the silencing of demons.

8:33 Get behind me, Satan. By urging Jesus to back away from his teaching about suffering and death, Peter is doing what Satan did: tempting Jesus with the promise that he can have the whole world without pain (Matt. 4:8–10).

8:34–38 Jesus defines what following him means. It involves denial, cross-bearing and losing one's life. The original recipients of the letter (the Christians in Rome) were doing this very thing: suffering for the sake of Jesus.

8:34 the crowd. This message is intended to be heard by everyone who wishes to follow Jesus. While the miracles might have made it appear that the kingdom of God simply meant fulfillment and joy, Jesus makes it clear that the way to the kingdom involves self-denial and sacrifice. Mark appears to have especially directed these words to the situation faced by the original recipients of the Gospel, the Christians in Rome who were in fact suffering for the sake of Jesus during the persecution under Nero. **deny himself/take up his cross/follow Me.** To "take up a cross" was something done only by a person sentenced to death by crucifixion, a reality that had faced some of the comrades of Mark's readers who had been executed by Nero. This stark image points out that to be a follower of Jesus means loyalty to him must precede all desires and ambitions, including the natural desire for self-preservation. Like Jesus, his followers are to single-mindedly pursue God's way even when it means suffering and death.

8:35 save his life. The image is of a trial in which one is called upon to renounce Jesus in order to live. This would have immediate application to the Christians in Rome who were pressed with the decision of considering whether to affirm their loyalty to Jesus and face the persecution of the state or deny their association with Jesus and be allowed to live. **will lose it.** That is, the person will ultimately face the judgment of God for his or her denial of Christ. **whoever loses his life ... will save it.** In this gospel, John the Baptist represents such a faithful person (6:14–29).

8:38 ashamed of Me. This would be indicated by failing to persist in one's Christian testimony in times of persecution. **adulterous and sinful generation.** This is reminiscent of the language of the Old Testament prophets who used adultery as a metaphor for Israel's disloyalty to God. **Son of Man/glory of His Father/holy angels.** This is apocalyptic imagery borrowed from Daniel 7:13ff. The Jewish expectation was that God's kingdom would one day be decisively and dramatically ushered in.

SESSION 8 : JESUS AND THE TRANSFIGURATION

SCRIPTURE MARK 9:2-13

LAST WEEK

In last week's session, we saw Jesus teaching his disciples about his role and purpose as the Messiah. We also considered what it means to "take up our cross" and be a true follower of Christ. Today we will focus on Jesus' transfiguration. This was a very spiritual moment for him and the disciples who were with him. We will examine the importance of this event and what it means to us today.

ICE-BREAKER : CONNECT WITH YOUR GROUP | 15 MINUTES

LEADER: Open with a word of prayer, and be sure to welcome and introduce new group members. Choose one, two or all three of the Ice-Breaker questions.

Mountaintop experiences: they're so exhilarating. And usually so short. Take turns sharing about some of your own "mountaintop" experiences.

1. What is your favorite thing to do on a mountain, and why?
   - ❏ Camping.
   - ❏ Hiking.
   - ❏ Skiing.
   - ❏ Hang gliding.
   - ❏ Other _____.

2. What is the highest mountain you have ever been on?

3. Where do you go to feel especially close to God?

In today's passage, Jesus has a special mountaintop experience with his disciples. Through this experience he fulfills prophecy and helps his disciples increase their understanding of who he is and what he has come to do. Let's read Mark 9:2–13 and try to understand the importance of this event.

The Transfiguration of Jesus

Mark: ²After six days Jesus took Peter, James, and John, and led them up on a high mountain by themselves to be alone. He was transformed in front of them, ³and His clothes became dazzling, extremely white, as no launderer on earth could whiten them. ⁴Elijah appeared to them with Moses, and they were talking with Jesus. ⁵Then Peter said to Jesus,

Peter: "Rabbi, it is good for us to be here! Let us make three tabernacles: one for You, one for Moses, and one for Elijah"–

Mark: ⁶because he did not know what he should say, since they were terrified.

⁷A cloud appeared, overshadowing them, and a voice came from the cloud: "This is My beloved Son; listen to Him!" ⁸Then suddenly, looking around, they no longer saw anyone with them except Jesus alone. ⁹As they were coming down from the mountain, He ordered them to tell no one what they had seen until the Son of Man had risen from the dead. ¹⁰They kept this word to themselves, discussing what "rising from the dead" meant.

¹¹Then they began to question Him,

Disciples: "Why do the scribes say that Elijah must come first?"

Jesus: ¹²"Elijah does come first and restores everything," He replied. "How then is it written about the Son of Man that He must suffer many things and be treated with contempt? ¹³But I tell you that Elijah really has come, and they did to him whatever they wanted, just as it is written about him."

Mark 9:2–13

QUESTIONS FOR INTERACTION

LEADER: Refer to the Summary and Study Notes at the end of this session as needed. If 30 minutes is not enough time to answer all of the questions in this section, conclude the Bible Study by answering question 7.

1. When have you experienced a powerful spiritual moment? What effect did it have on your life? Did you understand it at the time, or did you gain perspective later?

2. Why do you think Jesus took these men and created a smaller, more intimate group? Is this something we should be doing as a small group? How could it help our purpose?

3. What is the purpose of Elijah and Moses being present? What prophecy was fulfilled? Why did Peter want to build a tabernacle?

4. Why did Jesus tell them not tell anyone? Why do you think they still did not understand what "rising from the dead" meant?

5. If you had been there, what questions would you have been asking as you came down the mountain with Jesus?

6. How do you think Jesus (as a human) dealt with the anticipation of his suffering? What does the suffering Jesus went through mean to you?

7. God said "listen to Him." What do you need to hear Jesus say to you today?
   - ❏ I forgive you.
   - ❏ Open the door of your heart and let me in.
   - ❏ I will heal your pain.
   - ❏ You are my child.
   - ❏ I will take care of your needs.
   - ❏ Well done, faithful servant.
   - ❏ Other _____.

GOING DEEPER: If your group has time and/or wants a challenge, go on to this question.

8. How did Jesus answer the disciples' question about Elijah preceding the Messiah? How does Elijah's experience foreshadow Jesus' experience (see note on v. 13)?

CARING TIME : APPLY THE LESSON AND PRAY FOR ONE ANOTHER | 15 MIN.

LEADER: Have you discussed your group's mission–perhaps by sharing the vision of multiplying into two groups by the end of this study on the life of Christ?

Most of us have had "mountaintop" experiences in following Christ, times when he felt so close and his power seemed so real in our lives. But that is not the norm for most of us; we generally live in the valleys and only ascend the mountains from time to time. Gather around each other now for a time of sharing and prayer, learning to lean on one another as we live together in the valleys of life.

1. How would you best describe your relationship with God right now, and why?

2. Where are you suffering in your life right now?

3. How can the group pray for you regarding your answer to question 7?

NEXT WEEK

Today we looked at the mountaintop experience of the disciples as they witnessed the transfiguration of Jesus. We saw how Peter wanted to stay on the mountaintop, but Jesus brought him back to reality and stressed the importance of his mission. In the coming week, try to spend some extra time with God in prayer, and ask him for the strength and courage to carry out the mission he has planned for your life. Next time we will look at Jesus' last meal with his disciples.

Summary: The disciples have discovered that Jesus is no mere teacher (no matter how gifted and special he is), nor is he simply a prophet (no matter how powerful he might be). He is the Messiah—God's anointed Servant who has come to bring a new order in the world. Here in the Transfiguration, God affirms once again that Jesus is his beloved Son, and he declares to the people (through the three apostles who witness these events) that Jesus is, indeed, the Promised The account of the Transfiguration parallels in some interesting ways the baptism of Jesus (1:9–11). In the same way that the baptism of Jesus opened the first half of Mark (after some preliminary words from the Old Testament and from John the Baptist), the Transfiguration opens the second half (following some defining words by Jesus). In both incidents, the voice of God affirms that Jesus is his special Son. Both draw heavily on the Old Testament for their meaning. As the baptism of Jesus foreshadows his death, so the Transfiguration foreshadows his resurrection.

9:2 After six days. By this phrase Mark connects the Transfiguration with Jesus' prediction that "some of those standing here who will not taste death until they see the kingdom of God come in power" (9:1). The mention of "six days" is probably also an allusion to Exodus 24:15–18, where the story is told of Moses going up the mountain and remaining there six days until he is summoned into the presence of God. **Peter, James, and John.** These three emerge as an inner circle around Jesus. Mark has pointed out that Jesus took only these three disciples with him when he raised Jairus' daughter (5:37–41). Here he selects them to accompany him up the mountain. These are three of the first four disciples Jesus chose (1:14–20). **a high mountain.** This may well be Mount Hermon, a 9,000-foot mountain located some 12 miles from Caesarea Philippi (though early tradition says it is Mount Tabor, located southwest of the Sea of Galilee). The physical location of the mountain is not as significant as its theological meaning since mountains were the places in times past that God revealed himself to the leaders of Israel in special ways. For example, to Moses on Mount Sinai (Ex. 24) and to Elijah on Mount Horeb (1 Kin. 19). **transformed.** The word used here is **metamorphothe** (from which the English word "metamorphosis" comes). It means, literally, "to change one's form."

9:3 dazzling extremely white. The word "dazzling" (or "radiant") was used to describe the glistening of highly polished metal or the sparkling of sunlight. The phrase "white as snow" is found in Daniel 7:9, where it is used to describe the clothing of God when he appeared in a vision. Here the disciples witness Jesus being changed into a form just like God. In Revelation 1:9–18, the resurrected, glorified Jesus is described in similar terms. Brilliant, radiant light is often associated with appearances of God in the Old Testament.

9:4 Elijah. Elijah was a great prophet. The Jews expected that he would return just prior to the coming of the salvation they had been promised. And indeed, he is there on the mountain as the forerunner of the Messiah. **Moses.** The early Christians took this to be a prophecy about Jesus (Acts 3:22–26; 7:35–37). The presence of both Moses and Elijah on the mountain is meant to indicate that the Old Testament Law and the Prophets, which form the core of Israel's identity, endorse Jesus as God's appointed Messiah.

9:5 tabernacles. Peter might have had in mind the huts of intertwined branches which were put up at the Festival of Tabernacles to commemorate Israel's time in the wilderness. Or he might be thinking of the "tent of meeting" where God met with Moses. In making this suggestion, Peter shows his (quite understandable) confusion about this event. Did it mark the full arrival of the kingdom? Did this mean that Jesus had come into his glory without the suffering he told them about? How should he respond to such an amazing experience?

9:6 terrified. Throughout the Bible, whenever God is manifested before people, the human response is one of fear and of being undone (Ex. 3:5–6; 20:18–19; Judg. 6:20–23; Isa. 6:5; Dan. 10:7–8; Rev. 1:17).

9:7 This verse is full of allusions that are meant to confirm Jesus' divine authority. **A cloud.** The Old Testament often speaks of clouds as one of the phenomena which accompanies an appearance of God (Ex. 16:10; 19:9; 24:15–18; 40:34–38). Clouds are signs of his majesty and serve to veil his full glory from the eyes of mortals (who would otherwise be totally overwhelmed). This cloud is a symbol of the presence of God. **a voice.** Once again, as he did at the baptism of Jesus (1:11), God proclaims that Jesus is his Son. **This is my beloved Son.** By means of this event, it is revealed that not only is Jesus the Messiah (as the disciples have just confessed), he is also the Son of God. Both titles are necessary for a full understanding of his nature and role. As God's son, Jesus had the rights of heir and future King that even Moses and Elijah could never claim. **listen to him!** This is a quotation from Moses' prophecy about the coming prophet. The new prophet, whose authority and glory superseded that of Moses, was on the scene. This is a divine attestation to his authority, as well as the assertion that Jesus is more than a prophet.)

9:11 Elijah must come first. Since Elijah, a prophet who had called Israel to be faithful to God during a time of widespread apostasy, never died but was taken up into heaven by God (2 Kin. 2:1–2), the Jews believed that God would send Elijah back before the Messiah appeared to again call Israel to faithfulness (Mal. 4:5).

9:12 Elijah does come first. Here in the Transfiguration the long-expected Elijah comes. However, as verse 13 shows, Jesus asserts that Elijah has come in a second sense. John the Baptist came in the spirit and power of Elijah by being the forerunner of the Messiah. **How then is it written.** Jesus does not specify which Old Testament passage he has in mind, though a passage like Isaiah 53:3 would explain his statement here and in 8:31 that the Son of Man "must suffer" and die. While it seems incongruous to the disciples that the Messiah must suffer, Jesus reminds them that Elijah himself suffered at the hands of King Ahab and Queen Jezebel (1 Kin. 19:1–10).

9:13 Elijah really has come, and they did to him whatever they wanted, just as it is written about him. John the Baptist suffered and died at the hands of Herod and Herodias (6:14–29), paralleling Elijah's experience in the past. John's suffering and death foreshadow what awaits Jesus as well.

SESSION 9 : JESUS AND THE LAST SUPPER

SCRIPTURE MARK 14:12—26

LAST WEEK

The transfiguration of Jesus was our focus in last week's session. We saw the disciples grow in their understanding of Jesus and his mission, as a result of this event. We were also reminded to look to Jesus for guidance and "listen to Him" (9:7). Today we will observe the last meal Jesus had with his disciples, and consider what the Lord's Supper means to us today.

ICE-BREAKER : CONNECT WITH YOUR GROUP | 15 MINUTES

LEADER: Open with a word of prayer. Welcome and introduce new group members. Choose one, two or all three Ice-Breaker questions, depending on your group's needs.

Sharing a meal has always been an important time for people to share a bond and get to know each other better. In today's Scripture, Jesus uses a meal to create a bond between him and his disciples. This bond still exists among Christians today whenever they gather for the Lord's Supper. Share some of your thoughts and experiences with special meals.

1. What is one of your favorite places to eat?

2. If you were given a gift certificate for 12 for dinner, where would you take them, and why?

3. Growing up, what occasion did your family celebrate with a big meal? At whose house was it held? What was the main course?

LEADER: Select a member of the group ahead of time to read aloud the Scripture passage. Then discuss the Questions for Interaction, dividing into subgroups of three to six.

Jesus shares his last meal with the men he had called as his disciples more than three years earlier. Jesus had longed for this day because he knew it would be his last and everything was about to change. Read Mark 14:12–26, and note how the Lord's Supper helps us to remember what Jesus sacrificed for our salvation.

The Lord's Supper

¹²On the first day of Unleavened Bread, when they sacrifice the Passover lamb, His disciples asked Him, "Where do You want us to go and prepare the Passover so You may eat it?"

¹³So He sent two of His disciples and told them, "Go into the city, and a man carrying a water jug will meet you. Follow him. ¹⁴Wherever he enters, tell the owner of the house, 'The Teacher says, "Where is the guest room for Me to eat the Passover with My disciples?" ' ¹⁵He will show you a large room upstairs, furnished and ready. Make the preparations for us there." ¹⁶So the disciples went out, entered the city, and found it just as He had told them, and they prepared the Passover.

¹⁷When evening came, He arrived with the Twelve. ¹⁸While they were reclining and eating, Jesus said, "I assure you: One of you will betray Me—one who is eating with Me!"

¹⁹They began to be distressed and to say to Him one by one, "Surely not I?"

²⁰He said to them, "It is one of the Twelve—the one who is dipping bread with Me in the bowl. ²¹For the Son of Man will go just as it is written about Him, but woe to that man by whom the Son of Man is betrayed! It would have been better for that man if he had not been born."

²²As they were eating, He took bread, blessed and broke it, gave it to them, and said, "Take it; this is My body."

²³Then He took a cup, and after giving thanks, He gave it to them, and so they all drank from it. ²⁴He said to them, "This is My blood of the covenant, which is shed for many. ²⁵I assure you: I will no longer drink of the fruit of the vine until that day when I drink it new in the kingdom of God." ²⁶After singing psalms, they went out to the Mount of Olives.

Mark 14:12–26

QUESTIONS FOR INTERACTION

LEADER: Refer to the Summary and Study Notes at the end of this session as needed. If 30 minutes is not enough time to answer all of the questions in this section, conclude the Bible Study by answering questions 6 and 7.

1. How often do you partake in the Lord's Supper?
   - ☐ Weekly.
   - ☐ Monthly.
   - ☐ Quarterly.
   - ☐ Yearly.
   - ☐ No plan.
   - ☐ Spontaneously.
   - ☐ Other _____.

2. What is one of the most memorable communion experiences you have had? Why was it special?

3. How is the Lord's Supper related to the Passover and what preparations did this meal require (see notes on v. 12)?

4. How do you think the disciples felt about what Jesus said concerning the betrayer and the consequences of his betrayal (vv. 18–21)?

5. What profound new meaning does Jesus give to the Passover bread (v. 22) and to the Passover cup (vv. 23–24)?

6. Why is it important for Christians to observe Communion? What does the Lord's Supper mean to you?

7. Before you take Communion the next time, what can you do to make it more spiritually meaningful?

GOING DEEPER: If your group has time and/or wants a challenge, go on to this question.

8. What did the disciples experience in taking their first Communion that we have lost today? What is your church doing to recover the depth of this experience?

CARING TIME : APPLY THE LESSON AND PRAY FOR ONE ANOTHER | 15 MIN.

LEADER: Have you identified someone in the group that could be a leader for a new small group when your group divides? How could you encourage and mentor that person? You may want to consider the Lord's Supper as part of the Caring Time this week, depending on your church's policy.

For us to truly appreciate the Lord's Supper and Jesus' redemptive work, we need more than study—we need fellowship and the support of other Christians around us. This is your time to give that to each other. Share your responses to the following questions before closing in prayer.

1. What do you look forward to most about these meetings?

2. What is something for which you are particularly thankful?

3. How can the group pray for you as you seek to make the Lord's Supper more meaningful in your life?

NEXT WEEK

Today we looked at Jesus' last meal with his disciples. We saw how Jesus created this special meal for them and us, so we can remember the salvation Christ has brought us in his suffering and death. In the coming week, read 14:12–26 again and reflect on its meaning in your life. Next week we will look at Jesus' prayer in the Garden of Gethsemane. We will consider what it means to truly follow God's will, even when the way is difficult.

Summary: Through this meal, Jesus formally introduced the fact that his death was the means by which a new covenant was to be established between God and his people. It is this meal that declares Jesus' abiding presence with his people and gives meaning to Jesus' death as a sacrifice for sins. Just as at Passover a lamb was sacrificed as a means of atoning for the sins of the people, so Jesus' death is a sacrifice that leads God to "pass over" (or forgive) the sins of those who entrust themselves to him.

14:12 On the first day of Unleavened Bread. The Feast of Unleavened Bread did not officially start until the day after the Passover. However, in the first century, the day on which the lambs were sacrificed was sometimes referred to as the first day of the Feast of Unleavened Bread. **sacrifice the Passover lamb.** Each pilgrim sacrificed his own lamb in the temple. A priest caught the blood in a bowl and this was thrown on the altar. After removing certain parts of the lamb for sacrifice, the carcass was returned to the pilgrim to be roasted and eaten for Passover. Josephus estimated that 250,000 lambs were killed at Passover, turning the temple courts into a bloody mess. **prepare.** The disciples have to set out the unleavened bread and the wine (which was mixed with water) collect the bitter herbs (horseradish, chicory, etc.); make the sauce in which the bread was dipped (a stew of dried fruit, spices and wine); and roast the lamb on an open fire. **the Passover.** The meal began with a blessing and the first (of four) cups of wine. Psalms were then sung and the story of the deliverance read, followed by the second cup of wine and the eating of the bread, herbs, and the sauce (into which Judas and the others dip their bread–v. 20). Then the meal of roast lamb and bread is eaten. More prayers are said and the third cup is drunk. More psalms are sung; the final cup is drunk, after which a psalm is sung. Two short prayers end the feast.

14:13 a man carrying a water jug. Such a person would have been easy to spot and follow, since it was highly unusual for a man to carry a jug. Women carried jugs; men carried wineskins.

14:17 When evening came. The Passover meal could be eaten only after sunset. It was a night of excited watching in which people asked: "Will this be the night when God comes again to deliver his people from bondage?"

14:18-21 Jesus predicts that one of his disciples will betray him.

14:18 reclining. People would eat festive meals by lying on couches or cushions arranged around a low table. **I assure you.** Literally, this is "Amen," a word used to announce a solemn declaration.

14:20 dipping bread with Me into the bowl. To share in a meal was a sign of friendship, accenting the act of betrayal.

14:21 as it is written about Him. Passages such as Isaiah 53:1-6 point to the suffering of God's chosen servant. **woe to that man.** While the suffering of God's Messiah is part of God's plan, the people involved in that act are responsible for their decisions. **It would have been better for that man if he had not been born.** This is a stern warning of the judgment to come upon Judas (and others) who turn their backs on Jesus.

14:22 To share in the torn Passover bread, which Jesus reinterprets as his own person, is to share in his life, mission and destiny.

14:22 took bread, blessed and broke it, and gave it to them. Commonly at Passover, bread was broken and distributed prior to the meal as a reminder of how God had provided bread for his people in the wilderness. Jesus' action at this point in the meal would be unusual, calling attention to its new, special meaning. **this is My body.** Literally, "This, my body." While the bread used to represent God's provision of food for his people while they wandered in the wilderness, now it is to represent Jesus' body which was broken and torn upon the cross. To share in this bread is to affirm that one finds life in Jesus' sacrifice, is committed to his teaching, and shares in his mission.

14:23 cup. Jesus relates the Passover cup of red wine to the renewal of the covenant of God with his people via his sacrificial death.

14:24 covenant. In general terms, this is a treaty between two parties. Such an agreement was often sealed by the sacrifice of an animal. In specific terms, it refers to the arrangement that God made with Israel (Ex. 24:1–8), which was dependent on Israel's obedience. Now (as anticipated in Jer. 31:31–33) a new covenant is established, which is made dependent on Jesus' obedience (his sacrificial death). A covenant of law becomes a covenant of love. **shed.** Blood which was poured out symbolized a violent death (Gen. 4:10–11; Deut. 19:10; Matt. 23:35). This phrase points to the type of death Jesus would have. **for many.** This is an idiomatic expression meaning all people (10:45). The point is not that each and every individual will experience the benefits of the covenant regardless of their commitments, but that this is a covenant promise for all types of people throughout the world, not only for the Jews.

14:25 I will no longer drink. This may mean that Jesus chose to abstain from the fourth Passover cup which was passed around at the close of the meal, indicating that this Passover meal will only be consummated when Jesus ushers in God's kingdom in its fullness. **the kingdom of God.** The presence of God's reign was often pictured as a great banquet.

14:26 The Hallel (Ps. 113–118) was sung at the Passover; the first part (Ps. 113–114) prior to the meal and the second part, mentioned here, after the meal (Ps. 115–118). The rich promises of Psalm 118 would be on Jesus' lips as he leaves the room to face the Crucifixion only a few hours away. Think of Jesus singing Psalm 116, and then think of his cries in the Garden of Gethsemane. Moving on to Psalm 118, this is the psalm from which the familiar chorus "This is the day that the Lord has made" comes. The Day spoken of is the day that Christ makes atonement for the sins of the world and ushers in the way to eternal life.

SESSION 10 : JESUS IN GETHSEMANE

SCRIPTURE MARK 14:32-42

LAST WEEK

In last week's session, we looked at the last meal Jesus had with his disciples, which was the beginning of Communion as we know it today. We were reminded that this is an important way to remember what Christ did for us in his suffering and death, so we need to make the Lord's Supper as meaningful as possible. Today we will look at Jesus' prayer of agony in the Garden of Gethsemane, and see the example Jesus gives us in following God's will.

| ICE-BREAKER : CONNECT WITH YOUR GROUP | 15 MINUTES |

LEADER: Choose one or two of the Ice-Breaker questions. If you have a new group member, you may want to do all three. Remember to stick closely to the three-part agenda and the time allowed for each segment.

There's nothing quite so satisfying as a good night's sleep or a cozy afternoon nap. Of course, one can overdo it, and sometimes life's pressures force us to underdo it as well. The disciples found they could not stay awake and watch with Jesus in the Garden of Gethsemane. Take turns sharing some of your experiences with sleep.

1. What is the longest stretch of time you have stayed awake?

2. What do you do to keep yourself awake?
   - ☐ Take No Doze.
   - ☐ Drink lots of caffeine.
   - ☐ Play loud music.
   - ☐ Work.
   - ☐ Other _____.

3. What is the longest stretch of time you have slept?

BIBLE STUDY : READ SCRIPTURE AND DISCUSS | 30 MINUTES

LEADER: Select two members of the group ahead of time to read aloud the Scripture passage. Have one member read the part of Mark and the other the part of Jesus. Then discuss the Questions for Interaction, dividing into subgroups of three to six.

In today's passage, Jesus is facing the reality of taking on the sin of the world and being judged by the Father. It is impossible to imagine what it would be like to be responsible for all the guilt and sin of every human being. Let's read Mark 14:32-42 and try to understand what he did for us.

Jesus in Gethsemane

Mark: ³²Then they came to a place named Gethsemane, and He told His disciples,

Jesus: "Sit here while I pray."

Mark: ³³He took Peter, James, and John with Him, and He began to be horrified and deeply distressed. ³⁴Then He said to them,

Jesus: "My soul is swallowed up in sorrow—to the point of death. Remain here and stay awake."

Mark: ³⁵Then He went a little farther, fell to the ground, and began to pray that if it were possible, the hour might pass from Him. ³⁶And He said,

Jesus: "*Abba*, Father! All things are possible for You. Take this cup away from Me. Nevertheless, not what I will, but what You will."

Mark: ³⁷Then He came and found them sleeping.

Jesus: "Simon, are you sleeping?"

Mark: He asked Peter.

Jesus: "Couldn't you stay awake one hour? ³⁸Stay awake and pray, so that you won't enter into temptation. The spirit is willing, but the flesh is weak."

Mark: ³⁹Once again He went away and prayed, saying the same thing. ⁴⁰And He came again and found them sleeping, because they could not keep their eyes open. They did not know what to say to Him. ⁴¹Then He came a third time and said to them,

Jesus: "Are you still sleeping and resting? Enough! The time has come. Look, the Son of Man is being betrayed into the hands of sinners. ⁴²Get up; let's go! See—My betrayer is near."

Mark 14:32-42

QUESTIONS FOR INTERACTION

LEADER: Refer to the Summary and Study Notes at the end of this session as needed. If 30 minutes is not enough time to answer all of the questions in this section, conclude the Bible Study by answering questions 6 and 7.

1. What three friends would you call in a crisis?

2. Why did Jesus bring Peter, James and John to such an intimate setting with him?
   - ☐ He needed their support.
   - ☐ He was testing their endurance.
   - ☐ He wanted them to pray for him.
   - ☐ He knew they needed to pray for themselves.
   - ☐ Other _____.

3. What did Jesus ask God when he prayed? What do you learn about Jesus from this passage?

4. Why couldn't the disciples stay awake? What was the "temptation" (v. 38) Jesus was warning them about?

5. Jesus told Peter, "The spirit is willing, but the flesh is weak." How do these words apply to you?

6. What have you found helpful in determining God's will for your life?
   - ☐ Studying the Bible.
   - ☐ Praying.
   - ☐ Seeking counsel.
   - ☐ Attending church.
   - ☐ Other _____.

7. Where in your life do you need to submit to God's will?

GOING DEEPER: If your group has time and/or wants a challenge, go on to this question.

8. How was Jesus' statement "what You will" different from when we pray "your will be done"?

LEADER: Continue to encourage group members to invite new people to the group. Remind them that this group is for learning and sharing, but also for reaching out to others.

Jesus took Peter, James and John with him while he wrestled with the deep grief that he was feeling as he approached Calvary. There are times when we all need to have some brother or sister nearby just to pray for us while we go through deep grief or struggle. Use this group as a source for such support, and be available to others who may need your help.

1. Rate this past week on a scale of 1 (terrible) to 10 (great). What's the outlook for this week?

2. What friends in your life have been of great help and comfort to you? What people in this group have been that way?

3. What are you "deeply distressed" about? What bitter "cup" are you facing?

NEXT WEEK

Today we considered Jesus' prayer in the Garden of Gethsemane. We saw how he struggled with carrying the heavy burden of the sins of mankind. We also saw how disappointed he was when Peter, James and John couldn't even stay awake with him. In the coming week, spend an extra hour in prayer, even if it means getting up earlier or staying up later. Next week we will look at Jesus' trial before Pilate, and consider how his silence was a powerful witness.

Summary: This scene follows immediately after the Lord's Supper. Two themes dominate this section: Jesus' continued obedience to God despite his dread of what was coming, and the disciples' continued failure to grasp what lay ahead for Jesus.

14:32 Gethsemane. An olive orchard at the foot of the Mount of Olives just outside the eastern wall of Jerusalem. The name means literally, "an oil press" (for making olive oil).

14:33 Peter, James, and John. Once again, these three men accompany Jesus during a time of great significance. Interestingly, neither the rebuke of Peter (8:32) nor the self-centered request of James and John (10:35-40) has damaged their relationship with Jesus. Also, note that each of these men has vowed to stay with Jesus through thick or thin (10:38-39; 14:29,31). What Jesus asks them to share with him is not glory (which they wanted), but sorrow (which they kept denying would come). **deeply distressed.** Literally, filled with "shuddering awe." Jesus is filled with deep sorrow as the impact of submitting to God's will hits him.

14:34 stay awake. This was an invitation for the disciples to join him in preparation for the severe trial that was soon to come. While it expresses Jesus' desire for human companionship in his time of crisis, it also points out that these men need to prepare themselves as well. Verses 37-41 show that his concern was for how they would face the fact of his arrest and death.

14:35 a little farther. A few yards more. **fell to the ground.** This accents the emotional distress he was feeling. He is physically overwhelmed by the depth of sorrow and anxiety he feels. **pray.** It was customary at the time for people to pray aloud. Therefore, the disciples heard (and remembered) his prayer. This is the third time in Mark that Jesus has been shown in prayer (1:35; 6:46). **the hour.** This word is often used to refer to an event that represents a crucial turning point in God's plan for a person or for the world (13:32; 14:41). In reference to Jesus, it specifically refers to his crucifixion (John 12:23ff). Jesus' plea is that there might be some way for God's plan to be fulfilled without him having to face this particular "hour."

14:36 Abba. This is how a child would address his father: "Daddy." This was not a title that was used in prayer in the first century. **this cup.** Like the word "hour," "cup" was also used as an image referring to the destiny God had in store for a person. In some cases it refers to "the cup of salvation" the Lord gives his people to drink (Ps. 16:5; 116:13). **not what I will, but what You will.** This is the classic expression of Jesus' submission to God. While his personal desire was to avoid the cross, his deeper commitment was to do the Father's will even though it included the cross. For Jesus, this phrase is an expression of his final resolve. Although the prospect of the cross seemed crushing to him, this statement expresses his commitment to pursue God's will despite the cost.

14:37 sleeping. It was very late (the Passover could extend up to midnight), and they had drunk at least four cups of wine. **Simon, are you sleeping?** Jesus had earlier warned Peter that he would soon disavow ever having known Jesus, a charge Peter denied emphatically (vv. 29-31). Despite this warning, even Peter fails to prepare himself to face what was to come. **one hour.** This time the word is used literally. Despite Jesus' clear warning that a major crisis was coming, Peter and the other two disciples could not even take a relatively short amount of time to prepare themselves.

14:38 Stay awake and pray. This call to watch and pray echoes what is found in the parable about the owner of the house (13:35–37) referring to the time of the coming of the Son of Man in power and glory (13:26–27). It may be that Mark intends his readers to learn a lesson from the three disciples here. Their subsequent denial and desertion of Jesus indicates what happens to those who fail to prepare themselves spiritually. The owner of the house returns and the servants are not carrying out their tasks. In contrast, those who follow Jesus are to be spiritually awake at all times so they are not caught off guard when the times of trial and crisis arrive **temptation.** The trial or test that is about to come upon them is not merely something that might cause physical pain. It is one that could lead them to deny their loyalty to God himself. **The spirit is willing, but the flesh is weak.** The word "flesh" refers not simply to a person's body but one's human nature. It is an observation that although God's Spirit is available to help them, the orientation of their lives is still not toward God (Ps. 51:12).

14:40 They did not know what to say to Him. This is reflective of the householder's servants who are left without excuse when confronted with the fact that they have failed to carry out their duties faithfully (13:36). The disciples simply cannot grasp the pressing importance of the situation they face.

14:41 a third time. Jesus had earlier warned Peter that he would deny him three times (v. 30). Now Jesus comes to Peter three times to urge him to pray and become prepared for what is to come. However, as in the other two times, Peter and the others are asleep again. **Are you still sleeping and resting?** This is an ironic note of rebuke. Right up to the moment of crisis, the disciples fail to recognize what is happening. They have not prepared themselves at all. **into the hands of sinners.** This refers to the religious authorities that Jesus confronted in the previous section (11:1–13:37) who have corrupted the offices they hold. The irony of this assessment is that the term "sinners" was used by these religious leaders to refer to others: to Jews who did not live by the Law, and to all Gentiles. In fact, it is a term they have earned by their actions.

14:42 Get up: Let's go! Having resolved to do the Father's will, Jesus takes the initiative to approach the crowd coming to arrest him. This action illustrates the words of John's Gospel when Jesus declared, "No one takes it (my life) from Me, but I lay it down of My own" (John 10:18).

SESSION 11 : JESUS BEFORE PILATE

SCRIPTURE MARK 15:1–20

LAST WEEK

We were reminded of the great suffering that Jesus endured for us, as we saw his agony in the Garden of Gethsemane in last week's session. We also considered the example that Jesus gave us in following God's will, even when the circumstances are overwhelming. Today we will study Jesus' court appearance before the Roman leader, Pilate. We will continue to see the suffering that Jesus endured on our behalf.

ICE-BREAKER : CONNECT WITH YOUR GROUP | 15 MINUTES

LEADER: Open with a word of prayer. Choose one, two or all three Ice-Breaker questions, depending on your group's needs.

Life is filled with decisions, and one of the most difficult decisions is what to do when someone says false or hurtful things about us. Jesus chose to remain silent in his trial before Pilate. Take turns sharing your thoughts and experiences with times of false accusation and decision making.

1. When do you have trouble controlling your tongue?

2. When have you even been falsely accused? How did you react?

3. When do you have the hardest time making up your mind?
    - ❑ What to wear.
    - ❑ What to eat.
    - ❑ When to go to bed.
    - ❑ Where to vacation.
    - ❑ When to relax.
    - ❑ Other _____.

LEADER: Select three members of the group ahead of time to read aloud the Scripture passage. Then discuss the Questions for Interaction, dividing into subgroups of three to six.

Jesus' trial and suffering for our salvation continues. The night before this, Jesus had been arrested and brought before the Sanhedrin (Jewish high court). He was found guilty of blasphemy—a crime punishable by death. However, the Sanhedrin's power was limited by Roman rule; so now they bring Jesus to Pilate, the Roman governor, with a request for his execution. Let's read Mark 15:1-20 and get a picture of the last hours of Jesus' suffering.

Jesus before Pilate

Reader One:

15 As soon as it was morning, the chief priests had a meeting with the elders, scribes, and the whole Sanhedrin. After tying Jesus up, they led Him away and handed Him over to Pilate.

²So Pilate asked Him, "Are You the King of the Jews?"

He answered him, "You have said it."

³And the chief priests began to accuse Him of many things. ⁴Then Pilate questioned Him again, "Are You not answering anything? Look how many things they are accusing You of!" ⁵But Jesus still did not answer anything, so Pilate was amazed.

Reader Two:

⁶At the festival it was Pilate's custom to release for them one prisoner whom they requested. ⁷There was one named Barabbas, who was in prison with rebels who had committed murder in the rebellion. ⁸The crowd came up and began to ask Pilate to do for them as was his custom. ⁹So Pilate answered them, "Do you want me to release the King of the Jews for you?" ¹⁰For he knew it was because of envy that the chief priests had handed Him over. ¹¹But the chief priests stirred up the crowd so that he would release Barabbas to them instead.

¹²Pilate asked them again, "Then what do you want me to do with the One you call the King of the Jews?"

¹³And again they shouted, "Crucify Him!"

¹⁴Then Pilate said to them, "Why? What has He done wrong?" But they shouted, "Crucify Him!" all the more.

¹⁵Then, willing to gratify the crowd, Pilate released Barabbas to them. And after having Jesus flogged, he handed Him over to be crucified.

Reader Three:

¹⁶Then the soldiers led Him away into the courtyard (that is, headquarters) and called the whole company together. ¹⁷They dressed Him in a purple robe, twisted a crown out of thorns, and put it on

Him. ¹⁸And they began to salute Him, "Hail, King of the Jews!" ¹⁹They kept hitting Him on the head with a reed and spitting on Him. And getting down on their knees, they were paying Him homage. ²⁰When they had mocked Him, they stripped Him of the purple robe, put His clothes on Him, and led Him out to crucify Him.

Mark 15:1–20

QUESTIONS FOR INTERACTION

LEADER:Refer to the Summary and Study Notes at the end of this session as needed. If 30 minutes is not enough time to answer all of the questions in this section, conclude the Bible Study by answering question 7.

1. How do you think Jesus' trial would have played out on court TV? Was it the trial of the ages?

2. Why did the Jewish leaders bring Jesus to Pilate? What false accusations did they concoct?

3. Why do you think Jesus was so silent before Pilate?
   - ❑ His words had been so twisted against him there was no point in speaking.
   - ❑ He trusted God's plan.
   - ❑ The ears of his accusers were sealed against him.
   - ❑ The Old Testament prophesied the Messiah's silence before his accusers.
   - ❑ Other _____.

4. Why does Pilate give the Jewish leaders an audience? What do you think his impression is of Jesus?

5. How do you feel when you read verses 16–20? Who was this kind of punishment usually reserved for?

6. What does this episode of Jesus' life mean to you as his follower?

7. What can you do to stand by Jesus even when it is unpopular?

GOING DEEPER: If your group has time and/or wants a challenge, go on to this question.

8. What is symbolic of Barabbas' release instead of Jesus? How does this illustrate what Jesus did for us?

CARING TIME : APPLY THE LESSON AND PRAY FOR ONE ANOTHER | 15 MIN.

LEADER: Conclude the prayer time today by asking God for guidance in determining the future mission and outreach of this group.

Rejoice in what Jesus has done for you, and join in a time of sharing and prayer. After responding to the following questions, share prayer requests and close with a group prayer.

1. Have you been falsely accused or persecuted innocently? How can the group help you?

2. What can we do for Christians who are being persecuted in the world?

3. How can the group pray for you and your relationship with Jesus?

NEXT WEEK

Today we looked at Jesus before Pilate and saw how he faced his accusers in silence. We also saw the brutal suffering and punishment he went through in our place. We were reminded that there may be times when we suffer persecution for our faith, and we need to pray for strength and courage to face those times. In the coming week, take time each day to thank Jesus for all of the suffering he endured because of his unconditional love for you. Next week we will focus on the crucifixion of our Lord, and what that means for our salvation.

Summary: The Jewish trial is now followed by a Roman trial. The Jewish high court consisted of the 71 members of the Sanhedrin; the Roman court involved only one man. The trial before the Sanhedrin was conducted secretly, out of the eye of the public; the trial before Pilate was held openly in a public forum.

15:1 morning. The court began at daybreak, making it necessary that the Sanhedrin meet in an all-night session. They were anxious to get a quick conviction before the people found out what they had done. **had a meeting.** Legally, the Sanhedrin had no authority to order the death of Jesus (John 18:31). The real reason they defer to the Roman legal system (as Mark makes clear) is their fear of the people (11:32; 12:12; 14:1-2). However, the difficulty they faced is that under Roman law, blasphemy was not a capital offense. Consequently, they needed to present the case to Pilate so as to ensure Jesus' death. Their decision was that when they brought Jesus to Pilate, they would charge him with high treason. **led Him away.** They probably took him to the palace of Herod, located northwest of the temple, where Pilate stayed when he came to Jerusalem from his home in Caesarea. Pilate was probably in town for the feast. **Pilate.** Pontius Pilate was the fifth procurator of Judea. He served from A.D. 26-36. Historians of the time called him an "inflexible, merciless and obstinate" man who disliked the Jews and their customs.

15:2 King of the Jews. This is how the Sanhedrin translated the Jewish title "Messiah" so that Pilate would understand it. Put this way, it made Jesus seem guilty of treason (he would appear to be disputing the kingship of Caesar). **You have said it.** As he accepts the title "the Christ, the Son of the Blessed One" from the Jewish high priest (14:61-62), he also accepts the title "king of the Jews" from the Roman procurator.

15:3 accuse Him of many things. Luke 23:2,5 gives a sense of the kinds of charges the authorities made against Jesus. They accused him of opposing the payment of taxes to Rome, of stirring up people from Galilee and Judea to insurrection and of claiming to be the rightful king of the Jews. All of these things would be seen as a direct affront against Rome.

15:7 Barabbas. Nothing is known of Barabbas, but probably he was a prominent member of a failed revolt against Rome. Attacks against Roman authority were not uncommon in Judea, where people deeply resented Roman rule. The irony here is that this name means "son of the father." While rejecting the true Son of the Father, the authorities chose to free the very type of man they falsely accuse Jesus of being.

15:8 The crowd. It seems ironic that the crowd, who at the beginning of the week hailed Jesus as "He who comes in the name of the Lord" (11:9), could at the end of the week call for his crucifixion. In fact, it was very unlikely that this was the same crowd. There were several hundred thousand people in Jerusalem during the Passover. Jesus was arrested secretly, late at night. Now it is early the next morning. His supporters had little time to hear of his abduction, much less to arrive at the palace for his trial. A different group had gathered that morning. Possibly they were supporters of Barabbas (a hero to many), who wanted him released by means of the Passover amnesty (v. 6).

15:9 the King of the Jews. This is a deliberate jibe at the Jewish authorities. Pilate is willing to release the one claiming to be their king, for he sees no threat at all in Jesus. In this way, Pilate, in effect, minimizes the significance of the Jews as a threat to Rome.

15:13 Crucify Him! This was not so much a deliberate rejection of Jesus as it was a statement that they would not listen to Pilate's appeal for Jesus instead of Barabbas.

15:14 Why? What has He done wrong? By this Mark underscores the point that Jesus was innocent of all charges brought against him. Like the Suffering Servant of the Lord in Isaiah 53:9, Jesus "had done no violence, nor was any deceit in his mouth" (NIV).

15:15 released Barabbas. The death of Jesus (who is innocent) in the place of Barabbas (who is guilty) is a visual statement of the meaning of substitutionary atonement. It explains what Jesus meant in 10:45 when he said that he came to "give his life as a ransom for many." **flogged.** This was a terrible punishment. Soldiers would lash a naked and bound prisoner with a leather thong into which pieces of bone and lead had been woven. The flesh would be cut to shreds. **crucified.** Crucifixion was the most feared of all punishments in the first-century world. It was cruel in the extreme and totally degrading.

15:16–20 The soldiers mock Jesus as the Sanhedrin had done before them (14:65). Whereas the Sanhedrin mocked the idea that he was the Messiah, the soldiers mock the idea that he is king. This whole scene is full of the humiliation of God's Messiah being ridiculed and abused by the oppressors of God's people.

15:16 soldiers. Probably the troops that had accompanied Pilate on his trip from Caesarea.

15:17 a purple robe. This was a symbol of royalty.

SESSION 12 : JESUS' CRUCIFIXION

SCRIPTURE MARK 15:22–41

LAST WEEK

In last week's session, we considered Jesus' trial before Pilate. We saw how he was silent before his accusers and trusted in God to carry out his plan. We were also reminded of the unimaginable love that Jesus has for each of us, as he showed by the tremendous suffering he was willing to undergo for our salvation. Today we will focus on the crucifixion of Jesus and his final hours, and the difference that Jesus' death makes in the way we live our lives.

| ICE-BREAKER : CONNECT WITH YOUR GROUP | 15 MINUTES |

LEADER: Open with a word of prayer, and then have your group discuss one, two or all three of the Ice-Breaker questions.

Death is never an easy topic to discuss. Most of us want to avoid it entirely! But when we think of Jesus' death we can have hope and peace. Take turns sharing some of your own thoughts and experiences with death.

1. Whose death (other than Christ's) has affected you the most?

2. How do you feel deep down when you attend funerals and burials?

3. Do you wear or carry a cross? Why or why not?

LEADER: Select a member of the group ahead of time to read aloud the Scripture passage. Then discuss the Questions for Interaction, dividing into subgroups of three to six.

Jesus' whole purpose in coming to earth was to die on the cross. He was separated from God because he took our sin upon himself, and God cannot even look upon sin. But by dying he paid our debt, giving us the opportunity to be free from sin. Let's read Mark 15:22–41 with reverence as we think about our Lord's death for us.

Jesus' Crucifixion

²²And they brought Him to the place called *Golgotha* (which means Skull Place). ²³They tried to give Him wine mixed with myrrh, but He did not take it. ²⁴Then they crucified Him and divided His clothes, casting lots for them to decide what each would get. ²⁵Now it was nine in the morning when they crucified Him. ²⁶The inscription of the charge written against Him was:

THE KING OF THE JEWS

²⁷They crucified two criminals with Him, one on His right and one on His left. ²⁸So the Scripture was fulfilled that says: "And He was counted among outlaws." ²⁹Those who passed by were yelling insults at Him, shaking their heads, and saying, "Ha! The One who would demolish the sanctuary and build it in three days, ³⁰save Yourself by coming down from the cross!" ³¹In the same way, the chief priests with the scribes were mocking Him to one another and saying, "He saved others; He cannot save Himself! ³²Let the Messiah, the King of Israel, come down now from the cross, so that we may see and believe." Even those who were crucified with Him were taunting Him.

³³When it was noon, darkness came over the whole land until three in the afternoon. ³⁴And at three Jesus cried out with a loud voice, "*Eloi, Eloi, lemá sabachtháni* ?" which is translated, "My God, My God, why have You forsaken Me?"

³⁵When some of those standing there heard this, they said, "Look, He's calling for Elijah!" ³⁶Someone ran and filled a sponge with sour wine, fixed it on a reed, offered Him a drink, and said, "Let us see if Elijah comes to take Him down!"

³⁷But Jesus let out a loud cry and breathed His last. ³⁸Then the curtain of the sanctuary was split in two from top to bottom. ³⁹When the centurion, who was standing opposite Him, saw the way He breathed His last, he said, "This man really was God's Son!"

⁴⁰There were also women looking on from a distance. Among them were Mary Magdalene, Mary the mother of James the younger and of Joses, and Salome. ⁴¹When He was in Galilee, they would follow Him and minister to Him. Many other women had come up with Him to Jerusalem.

Mark 15:22–41

QUESTIONS FOR INTERACTION

LEADER: Refer to the Summary and Study Notes at the end of this session as needed. If 30 minutes is not enough time to answer all of the questions in this section, conclude the Bible Study by answering question 7.

1. Have you ever sat with someone who was dying? What was it like?

2. What do you think of the method of crucifixion Jesus went through? How does the way he died affect how you feel about him? Your salvation?

3. Why did Jesus feel forsaken by God? When have you felt forsaken by God? Does it compare to what Jesus felt?

4. What is the significance of the curtain in the sanctuary being torn? How would you describe the curtain between you and God right now?
   - ❏ Wide open.
   - ❏ Half open.
   - ❏ Barely open.
   - ❏ Closed tight.
   - ❏ Other _____.

5. Who are the women at the cross? What is the significance of their presence and the disciples' absence?

6. How would you explain the spiritual implications of Jesus' death to someone who was considering becoming a follower of Christ?

7. When did the Crucifixion begin to make a difference in your life?
   - ❏ When I understood my sins were forgiven.
   - ❏ When I felt the peace of God in my life for the first time.
   - ❏ When I was able to forgive others.
   - ❏ When I committed my life to following Jesus.
   - ❏ Other _____.

GOING DEEPER: If your group has time and/or wants a challenge, go on to this question.

8. Why were some people thinking that Jesus was calling Elijah (v. 35)? What is the significance of this?

CARING TIME : APPLY THE LESSON AND PRAY FOR ONE ANOTHER | 15 MIN.

LEADER: Following the Caring Time, discuss with your group how they would like to celebrate the last session next week. Also, discuss the possibility of splitting into two groups and continuing with another study.

Come together now and encourage one another with the hope that Jesus has given us through his death and resurrection. Begin by sharing your responses to the following questions. Then share prayer requests and close in a group prayer.

1. What can you do in the coming week to encourage someone who doubts that Jesus can forgive his or her sins?

2. What healing do you still need from the loss of a loved one to death? How can the group pray for you for healing from this loss?

3. How can this group be supportive of you as you share with others what Jesus has done in your life?

NEXT WEEK

Today we looked at the crucifixion of our Lord, and considered how Jesus' death provides the only payment for our sins. Fortunately, the death of Christ is only half of the story; he not only died, but he defeated death permanently and rose again. In the coming week, follow through on your answer to question 1 during the Caring Time, and bring that hope into another person's life. Next week we will look at Jesus' glorious resurrection and the implications for the entire human race.

Summary: Here, the Son of Man truly gives his life as a ransom for many (10:45), fulfilling God's plan (14:36). While the death of Jesus has been the event that Mark has looked toward throughout his gospel, when it actually happens he records it in a simple, stark way. The story of the death of Jesus is rich with allusions to Psalms 22 and 69 and Isaiah 53. These allusions and images indicate that the description in Mark is more than an actual account of the Crucifixion itself. It is a pictorial interpretation of the significance of Jesus' death as understood through the Old Testament prophecies.

15:22 Golgotha. In Aramaic, "a skull." This was possibly a round, bare hill outside the city wall of Jerusalem.

15:23 wine mixed with myrrh. It was a Jewish custom to offer this pain-deadening narcotic to prisoners about to be crucified (Ps. 69:21).

15:24 they crucified Him. Josephus, the Jewish historian, calls crucifixion "the most wretched of all ways of dying." The person to be crucified was first stripped. Then his hands were tied or nailed to the crossbeam. This was lifted to the upright stake, and then the feet were nailed in place. In the end it was death by asphyxiation, when the pain torn limbs could no longer raise the body to draw another breath into the oxygen starved lungs. **divided His clothes.** The clothes of the condemned person belonged to the four soldiers who carried out the crucifixion (Ps. 22:18; John 19:23-24).

15:26 The inscription. The crime for which the person was being crucified was specified on a whitened board fastened above the criminal. **THE KING OF THE JEWS.** By posting this sign on the cross, Pilate was simply attempting to further humiliate the Jews. The intent was to communicate that Jesus' fate would be shared by anyone else who tried to assert their authority against Rome.

15:27 criminals. This was a term sometimes used for Zealots, the band of nationalists who were committed to the violent overthrow of Rome. While "robbery" per se was not a capital crime, insurrection was. Perhaps they were involved with Barabbas in the incident mentioned in 15:7. In any case, the reference to being crucified alongside criminals is probably an allusion to Isaiah 53:12. **one on His right and one on His left.** Earlier on, James and John had asked to sit at Jesus' right and left hand when he came into his kingdom (10:37), a request Jesus denied. That position was left for these two criminals who shared in Jesus' death, the true means by which he would enter into his glory.

15:29 who would demolish the sanctuary and build it in three days. This claim is not made by Jesus in Mark's gospel, but it is found in John 2:19, where it is treated as a prophecy of his death and resurrection.

15:31 He saved others ... He cannot save Himself. This is just the point! Because he is saving others, his own life is forfeited. Once again Mark uses irony. Something true is said about Jesus by a person who does not understand the accuracy of the statement (14:61-62; 15:2).

15:32 Even those who were crucified with Him were taunting Him. Luke recounts how one of these men stopped his abuse and professed faith in Jesus as the Messiah (Luke

23:40–43). Mark's interest is in showing the depth of the rejection and abuse Jesus encountered right up to his death.

15:33 darkness. This phenomenon is mentioned in Matthew 27:45–46 and Luke 23:44–49. Luke adds, "The sun stopped shining." This would have been a terrifying and memorable event. Surely John recalled this when he wrote down the words about the New Jerusalem. "The city does not need the sun or the moon to shine on it, because God' glory illuminates it, and its lamp is the Lamb" (Rev. 21:23). How fitting that it should be dark when the Lamb of God was being sacrificed for the sins of the whole world.

15:35 Elijah. The people misunderstood what Jesus said. They thought he was calling upon the ancient prophet, Elijah. This is another ironic note, since Elijah had already come in the person of John the Baptist

15:36 Let us see if Elijah comes to take Him down! According to 2 Kings 2, Elijah never died; he was taken up into heaven by angels. The expectation was that Elijah would one day reappear to proclaim the advent of God's Messiah. Some in the crowd may have expected they were about to witness an eleventh hour vindication of Jesus.

15:37 a loud cry. This is unusual. Generally the victim is exhausted and unconscious at the point of death. Perhaps Mark is remembering Jesus cry, "It is finished" (John 19:30). In John 10:17 Jesus has clearly told his disciples that he lays down his life of his own accord, and that he takes it up again. This echoes the ending of Psalm 22, which asserts that as future generations tell their children about the Lord, they will declare that "he has done it." Jesus' work of securing salvation for humanity is accomplished.

15:38 curtain of the sanctuary. Three of the four gospels mention this event. According to the Law, only the High Priest could go into the Holy of Holies. But when Jesus, the perfect sacrifice, died, the way was opened for us to "enter the Most Holy Place by the blood of Jesus. (Heb. 10:19–20)

15:39 centurion. The supervising officer, probably a pagan soldier who may not or may not have been aware of the significance of what he observed. As Jesus himself stated, his ministry was not done in secret. It is intriguing to remember that his death could purchase eternal life for the very soldiers who crucified him. **God's Son.** This confession concludes the second half of Mark's gospel. In 1:1, Mark stated that what he was writing was the good news about Jesus the Messiah, the Son of God. The first half of the gospel ends with the confession of Peter (a Jew) that Jesus is the Messiah (8:29); the second half ends with the confession of the centurion (a Gentile) that Jesus is the Son of God. In this context, this confession is an affirmation of the deity of Jesus.

15:40 also women. Mark names three eyewitnesses of the Crucifixion. Mary Magdalene was from the village of Magdala on the west coast of Galilee (Luke 8:2). The other Mary had well-known sons in the early church. Salome was the wife of Zebedee and the mother of James and John (Matt. 27:56). In contrast, all the disciples have fled.

SESSION 13 : THE RESURRECTION OF JESUS

SCRIPTURE MATTHEW 28:1—20

LAST WEEK

The brutal crucifixion of Jesus was our topic in last week's session. We saw how Jesus sacrificed everything, even God's presence, to provide the only acceptable payment for our sins. We were encouraged to share this unconditional love of Jesus with others, and spread the hope that his death brings. In this, our final study on the life of Christ, we will discover that Jesus went beyond defeating sin by defeating death itself.

ICE-BREAKER : CONNECT WITH YOUR GROUP | 15 MINUTES

LEADER: Begin this final session with a word of prayer and thanksgiving for this time together. Choose one or two Ice-Breaker questions to discuss.

Jesus' resurrection was a complete surprise to his followers. They still hadn't understood his ultimate purpose in coming to earth. Take turns sharing some of your thoughts and experiences with surprising circumstances.

1. What recent news story has been especially surprising to you and hard to believe?

2. How would you react if you were visiting a graveyard and an angel suddenly appeared?

3. What type of natural disaster has caught you unprepared and surprised? What happened?

LEADER: Select three members of the group ahead of time to read aloud the Scripture passage. Assign the following parts: Matthew (the narrator), Angel and Jesus. Ask the whole group to read the part of the chief priests in verses 13–14. Then discuss the Questions for Interaction, dividing into subgroups of three to six. Be sure to save some extra time at the end for the Caring Time.

Jesus did not stay in the tomb, despite the best efforts of the guards! His resurrection is the defining point of our salvation. Without his death and resurrection, Christianity is a lost cause and we are all doomed to an eternity apart from God. Thank God the story did not end at the Cross. Let's read Matthew 28:1–20 and rejoice in what Jesus has done for us.

The Resurrection of Jesus

Matthew: **28** After the Sabbath, as the first day of the week was dawning, Mary Magdalene and the other Mary went to view the tomb. [2]Suddenly there was a violent earthquake, because an angel of the Lord descended from heaven and approached the tomb. He rolled back the stone and was sitting on it. [3]His appearance was like lightning, and his robe was as white as snow. [4]The guards were so shaken from fear of him that they became like dead men. [5]But the angel told the women,

Angel: "Don't be afraid, because I know you are looking for Jesus who was crucified. [6]He is not here! For He has been resurrected, just as He said. Come and see the place where He lay. [7]Then go quickly and tell His disciples, 'He has been raised from the dead. In fact, He is going ahead of you to Galilee; you will see Him there.' Listen, I have told you."

Matthew: [8]So, departing quickly from the tomb with fear and great joy, they ran to tell His disciples the news. [9]Just then Jesus met them and said,

Jesus: "Rejoice!"

Matthew: They came up, took hold of His feet, and worshiped Him. [10]Then Jesus told them,

Jesus: "Do not be afraid. Go and tell My brothers to leave for Galilee, and they will see Me there."

Matthew: [11]As they were on their way, some of the guards came into the city and reported to the chief priests everything that had happened. [12]After the priests had assembled with the elders and agreed on a plan, they gave the soldiers a large sum of money [13]and told them,

Chief Priests:	"Say this, 'His disciples came during the night and stole Him while we were sleeping.' [14]If this reaches the governor's ears, we will deal with him and keep you out of trouble."
Matthew:	[15]So they took the money and did as they were instructed. And this story has been spread among Jewish people to this day. [16]The 11 disciples traveled to Galilee, to the mountain where Jesus had directed them. [17]When they saw Him, they worshiped, but some doubted. [18]Then Jesus came near and said to them,
Jesus:	"All authority has been given to Me in heaven and on earth. [19]Go, therefore, and make disciples of all nations, baptizing them in the name of the Father and of the Son and of the Holy Spirit, [20]teaching them to observe everything I have commanded you. And remember, I am with you always, to the end of the age."

Matthew 28:1–20

QUESTIONS FOR INTERACTION

LEADER: Refer to the Summary and Study Notes at the end of this session as needed. If 30 minutes is not enough time to answer all of the questions in this section, conclude the Bible Study by answering questions 6 and 7.

1. How do the women, the guards and the chief priests react to the news of the Resurrection?

2. What would be your reaction to seeing Jesus after leaving his tomb? How does Jesus validate the disciples' act of worship?

3. The disciples had abandoned Jesus but he had not abandoned them (v. 10). What does this say about Jesus' grace, love and forgiveness?

4. Why did the chief priest and elders want to spread the rumor that Jesus' disciples came and stole his body?

5. What is the central command Jesus gives his disciples? How is that command to be carried out? What is your role in that command?

6. What is the key thing you have learned in this study on the life of Christ?

7. How does the Great Commission affect what you will do with your life as a follower of Christ?

GOING DEEPER: If your group has time and/or wants a challenge, go on to this question.

8. How would you answer the arguments that: (a) the disciples stole Jesus' body; (b) the cool of the tomb revived Jesus and/or (c) the disciples made up this tale of the Resurrection?

CARING TIME : APPLY THE LESSON AND PRAY FOR ONE ANOTHER | 15 MIN.

LEADER: As you gather for what may be the last time this particular group is assembled, plan an extra amount of time for people to share more than usual. Lay hands on one another and commission each other to "Go, therefore, and make disciples of all nations" (v. 19). Pray for God's blessing in any plans to start a new group or to continue studying together.

The death of Jesus is only half the story. If he had stayed in the tomb, he would have been subject to the power of death in the same way that sinners are. When he rose again, he proved once and for all that he has power over elements of our world, even the greatest power of all—death. Spend some time together thanking God for his wonderful plan of redemption, and pray for guidance about what the group should do next.

1. What was your serendipity (unexpected blessing) during this course?

2. On a scale of 1 (baby steps) to 10 (giant leaps), how has your relationship with Christ progressed during the course of this study?

3. How would you like the group to continue to pray for you?

Summary: The story of Jesus ends not with his death but with his resurrection. After Jesus died on the cross, his body was removed and placed in the tomb of Joseph, a member of the Sanhedrin who had opposed the action of the council (27:57-61). The other council members, recalling how Jesus had predicted that he would rise from the dead, asked Pilate to post a guard around the tomb so that Jesus' disciples would not be able to steal the body and claim that Jesus had risen from the dead (27:62-66).

28:1 the first day of the week was dawning. The Sabbath was considered over at 6 p.m. on Saturday. This scene takes place early on Sunday morning. This is why Christians developed the tradition of worshiping on Sunday instead of on the Sabbath (Saturday). **Mary Magdalene and the other Mary.** While some of the Gospels mention other women who went to the tomb, all four Gospels place Mary Magdalene in a prominent role. Mark mentions that the women brought aromatic oils to anoint the body, not so much to preserve it as to honor it (much like people today would put flowers on a grave). Clearly they did not expect Jesus to have risen from the dead, since they were shocked by what they found.

28:2 earthquake. Earthquakes were often associated with manifestations of God's power (Hab. 3:6). **the stone.** A tomb like this was cut out of the side of a hill. A large disc-shaped stone was set in a groove so that it could be fairly easily rolled down to the opening to close it off. However, once in place it would have been very difficult for people to push it back up the incline.

28:6 He has been resurrected. In the same way that the Gospel writers report the crucifixion of Jesus in simple, stark terms (27:35; Mark 15:24), so, too, they describe the Resurrection in a plain, unadorned way. The phrase literally reads "he has been raised," showing that God is the one who accomplished this great act. Jesus' resurrection demonstrates that the cry of the centurion was accurate (27:54). **Come and see the place where He lay.** Typically such tombs had a large antechamber, with a small two-foot-high doorway at the back which led into the six- or seven-foot burial chamber proper. The stone was rolled away not so that the resurrected Jesus could leave the tomb (he was already gone), but so that his disciples could see that it was empty (John 20:8).

28:7 go/tell. Under Jewish law, women were not considered reliable witnesses. That they were the first to know of Jesus was an indication of how Christianity changed the way the whole world viewed women. The disciples are not ashamed to tell their incredulity (Luke 24:11,22-24), hence reinforcing that this detail is historically accurate. (They certainly would not have invented the story this way.) **His disciples.** They may have abandoned Jesus but he has not abandoned them! Mark records that a special word was given to Peter. After his abysmal failure, Peter might have been tempted to count himself out of further discipleship. **to Galilee.** Jesus said he would meet them again in Galilee (26:32). The ministry of Jesus and the Twelve began in Galilee and now they are directed back there to meet the risen Lord, thus bringing the account full circle.

28:8 with fear and great joy. This stands in contrast to Mark's gospel which states that the women "said nothing to anyone, because they were afraid" (Mark 16:8). As the realization that their beloved teacher was indeed alive, joy burst upon them and overcame their fear.

28:9 Jesus met them. While it differs in details, John records a similar appearance of Jesus to Mary Magdalene (John 20:16–17). **worshiped Him.** It is significant that it is twice mentioned after the Resurrection that people worshiped Jesus (v. 17). Whereas an angel rebukes John the apostle for bowing down to worship him (Rev. 22:8–9), Jesus accepts their worship. Since Jesus himself affirmed that only God should be worshiped (4:10), this is a clear acknowledgment of his divinity. As Paul wrote, the Resurrection was a demonstration of God's power affirming Jesus as the Son of God (Rom. 1:4).

28:13 Say this. While verses 19–20 tell of Jesus' commission to his disciples, this is the Sanhedrin's commission to the guards. The disciples are motivated and encouraged in their task by the living presence of Jesus (v. 20), while the guards are motivated only by money. **His disciples ... stole Him while we were sleeping.** This attempt at "damage control" was weak. The very reason the guards were posted was to keep the disciples from being able to steal the body and concoct a story about resurrection. From a longer-term perspective, it would be hard to believe that disciples who had stolen Jesus' body–and hence knew that the Resurrection was a hoax–would then go on to die for their faith, often in painful ways.

28:17 some doubted. So stupendous, and without precedent is the resurrection of Jesus that right from the beginning his disciples had difficulty accepting it. When the women reported what had happened at the tomb, the Eleven said that it sounded like nonsense (Luke 24:9–11). After 10 of the disciples (all but Thomas) met the resurrected Jesus and believed (Luke 24:36–48), Thomas still doubted (John 20:24–29). But upon seeing the wounds from the crucifixion, Thomas' response is unequivocal: "My Lord and my God!"

28:18 All authority has been giving to Me in heaven and on earth. This is the meaning of the statement "Jesus is Lord." Since there is no power greater than his (Rom. 8:38–39; Phil. 2:9–11; Col. 1:15–20), there is no other loyalty to which his disciples can give their absolute allegiance.

28:19 therefore. In light of Jesus' authority, he sends his people on a mission. **make disciples.** Literally, this is "as you are going, make disciples." The point is not so much that the apostles are to travel far and wide, but that as they go about their business (whatever that is and wherever it takes them), they are to be teaching people about Jesus and his kingdom. This is to be their pressing concern. **baptizing them.** Baptism was a sign of discipleship and faith. **in the name of the Father and of the Son and of the Holy Spirit.** This is a clear Trinitarian formula. While the doctrine of the Trinity was not clearly articulated and defined until the third century, the roots of its teaching are clearly seen here. There is one name (or character) that defines the triune God. To be baptized "in his name" (literally, "into the name") means to enter into fellowship with him.

28:20 teaching them to observe everything I have commanded you. The stress here is on the ethical dimensions of Christian living. Discipleship is practicing the way of life advocated and exemplified by one's master. **I am with you always.** This is the climactic promise of the new covenant. The presence of God with his people was always the goal toward which Israel looked under the old covenant. In Jesus, that presence is assured through the indwelling of Christ's Spirit (John 14:16–17). **to the end of the age.** This covers all time until the return of Christ when the new heaven and the new earth will be revealed.

personal notes

Personal Notes

PERSONAL NOTES

Personal notes

PERSONAL NOTES

Personal Notes